DOS Secrets

by Dan Gookin

Edited by Tina Rathbone
Cover illustration by Randy Verougstraete
Art direction by Kay Thorogood

First Edition Copyright © 1990
Computer Publishing Enterprises
P.O. Box 23478
San Diego, CA 92193
Toll Free (800) 544-5541

0-945776-12-8
10 9 8 7 6 5 4

ACKNOWLEDGEMENTS

I would like to thank Jack Dunning, Scott Millard, and Tina Berke of Computer Publishing Enterprises for letting me work on this book. Thanks also goes to Ken Bibb, who did original work on the *DOS Secrets* title.

To Ryan Gale, my own DOS guru
and perhaps the most fascinating
person I've ever met.

You died too young.

CONTENTS

INTRODUCTION

What Are "DOS Secrets?" Primarily, DOS secrets are those things that make using your computer easier. That hidden knowledge, those little tidbits of information that you just can't find anywhere—unless you look. Because there really are no secrets about DOS.

Most of the information about DOS, as well as other computer software, can be found in the manual. The problem is, manuals usually hide that information, or they list a feature but don't explain how to fully use it. You read the manual and think, "Oh, that's neat," and then move on, not knowing how what you've read could really help you.

That's where this book comes into play.

WHAT THIS BOOK IS ABOUT

A lot of DOS-type books are mere reprints of the DOS manual. They'll list DOS commands and functions and explain how each one works. But they don't tell you how to *use* the function. That's where this book is different.

Rather than a reprint of the DOS manual, this book is a collection of expert tips for using DOS. This sounds like it could be a pretty cryptic topic. Or worse, it could be material way beyond the reach of the average DOS user. But that's not the case here.

All the information presented here is really basic stuff. The problem is, no one's ever pointed it out to you before. DOS isn't that complex of an operating system. Your word processor has dozens more features and your spreadsheet is many levels more complex.

DOS is the most important piece of software you have on your PC. Yet few people really get the most out of it. Granted, you don't really have to. But when you do, you'll be able to work the computer more effectively, get work done faster, and know more about your PC. That makes you a better PC user and, in the office, a more valuable employee.

WHO ARE YOU?

This isn't a beginning book on DOS. Even though DOS is a secret mystery to anyone who first buys a PC, other books should be considered for a beginner (such as Computer Publishing Enterprises' *Beginner's Guide to DOS*).

To get the most out of this book, you should be an experienced DOS user. That's neither a beginning, intermediate, nor advanced level. It's something you can decide. Are you an experienced DOS user? Do you know your A drive from your B drive? Can you COPY files? Know a few DOS commands? If so, you qualify.

CONVENTIONS

No book on a computer topic, especially DOS, is complete without a few conventions. This book is no exception.

Because there are so many variations in computer lingo, this book will use the following general terms to apply to the diversity of DOS computer systems out there. This way, no one will be left out in the cold:

DOS Is DOS

There are two flavors of DOS: MS-DOS and PC-DOS. This book uses the term DOS to apply to both. The differences between MS-DOS and PC-DOS are slight. PC-DOS was designed to work specifically with IBM's computers, and it contains the BASIC programming language which will only work on IBM systems. Other than that, besides a few other technical issues, DOS is DOS.

DOS Versions

This book writes to the common base of DOS version 3.3. DOS version 4 has been out some time now, but still hasn't caught on as a mandatory upgrade. For that reason, it's documented here along with DOS 3.3 but noted as "DOS 4 only" where applicable. Some earlier versions of DOS may not have all the commands listed here for DOS 3.3. (You should really upgrade to 3.3 if you haven't already.)

Your Computer is a PC

All computers that run DOS are called PCs in this book. PC means Personal Computer. Traditionally, PC referred to the original IBM PC and PC/XT systems. There are also PC-AT systems and 386 computers that run DOS. Though each of these types of computer are at different performance levels and should be treated differently, this book refers to all systems as PCs. Any exceptions will be noted.

ENTER and RETURN

Most PC keyboards now have an ENTER key. Older systems may also have a RETURN key. This is the same key, referenced as ENTER in this book. ENTER is used to end a line of text, to input it in the computer. (In a word processor, ENTER ends a paragraph.) ENTER evolved from the calculator lineage of computers. RETURN, still used on some keyboards, evolved from electric typewriters.

Shift-Modifier Keys

The PC has three dead keys that are used to modify other keys. They are Shift, Control and Alt. When this book tells you to press Control-A, it means to press the Control shift-modifier key and type an A—just as you'd type Shift-A to produce a capital A.

^ Means Control

The hat character, ^, is used to indicate the Control key in many instances. When you see ^C, it means to type Control-C—or it means the character produced when Control-C is typed.

In addition to these conventions, while using this book you'll actually be entering commands at the DOS prompt. For the most part, these are DOS commands that were included on the DOS diskettes you got with your computer.

All DOS commands should be on your system's path. Otherwise, when you type in an example, you may get a "Bad command or filename" or "File not found" error. To avoid this, put your DOS subdirectory on the path. If that sounds confusing, then start reading this book at Chapter Four and then Chapter Six.

BETWEEN THE COVERS

This book contains nine chapters, which can be read in any order. Each chapter does follow the previous one in a logical fashion. However, there may be certain subjects you feel a good grasp of. In that case, you can skim or skip any chapter at your leisure.

There are four appendixes here, which provide ample reference for using some DOS secrets on your own.

Be aware that this book isn't an end-all to DOS secrets. It will just open the door a bit, allowing you to see some of the interesting things your computer's operating system is capable of. Other books will cover specific subjects here in detail, including the subjects of hard-disk management, computer programming, and DOS as a reference guide. But if you have all those books and they still don't tell you what you need to know, then you're reading the right tome.

Enjoy it!

PART ONE

CHAPTER 1

What Is a DOS Guru?

You've heard of the infamous DOS guru. They're the one you turn to whenever you need help, can't understand or don't want to understand a command—basically you just want to get the job done.

But what are they? How did they get that way? What's the secret?

A DOS guru is someone who knows how to use the MODE command.

DOS gurus are also those who really get to know their machine. They may do it because they want to do it, or simply because they're bored. Basically, they like to fiddle. By exploring you can learn a lot about your computer. Typing in each command, pressing each possible key—these all lead to certain results. So, I guess a DOS guru must also have patience and guts to be willing to try things like that.

This chapter is about those things that compose your typical DOS guru. Yeah, it sounds like a general topic, and there are five general sections to go with it:

- Knowing more than just how to use the computer

- Your user level

- Knowledge of terms

- PC styles
- How to find DOS secrets

This is basically a collection of stuff that all deals with your PC IQ, level of familiarity, and willingness to become what's commonly called a "DOS guru." Are you ready?

KNOWING MORE THAN JUST HOW TO USE THE COMPUTER

There are many reasons to learn more about your computer. The most important is that by using the system to its full capability, you're getting the most out of it. Also, the system is getting the most out of you. Once you know everything that the computer is capable of (or nearly everything), you'll be better able to express your thoughts using the computer.

No extra math or major in rocket science is necessary here. Though computers are often linked with those we knew in school as "Vulcans," there is very little involved in using a computer. More important than math (or computer science) is incentive.

You just don't become a DOS guru. You have to be willing to try. In order to become a DOS guru, you need incentive. If you naturally take to the concept of computers, you're in there.

And, needless to say, the benefits of being a guru far outweigh those of being a yellow-pad-head (see the next section). Besides getting the most out of your system, you'll become a successful expert in the field. Co-workers will ask you questions—even the boss! Being such a valued employee is something you should consider come raise time.

YOUR USER LEVEL

I consider that there are three levels of computer user. Or, as I call them, the Three Weenies:

- Total Weenie
- Weenie
- DOS Weenie

A Total Weenie is the worst type of computer user. Face it, computers aren't for everyone. Just as not everyone on the planet will ever learn or need to know how to fly an airplane, not everyone needs to know how to work a computer. (I propose that at some day these people be flagged for possible employment disadvantages; people can't learn to use a computer like they learn how to type.)

The Total Weenie person is usually easy to spot. They're the ones who keep the yellow pads of notes by their computers. When the DOS expert tells them what to do, they jot down notes. Or, as most gurus put it, they don't listen, they take notes.

This type of computer person will never ever learn how to use their system. They don't even try to *understand* what's going on. Instead, they'll always rely upon that yellow pad full of notes. Even though they may do the same thing, day after day, year after year at the same job, this person will still refer to the same notes that they took the first day on the job. (Trust me, I *know* people like this.)

The Weenie isn't as bad as the Total Weenie. In fact, most companies claim they have a DOS guru when in fact they only have a Weenie.

Unlike the Total Weenie, the Weenie doesn't need to take notes. They'll read the manuals (maybe, once) and they'll know how to do things like copy and rename files. They're quite adept at installing new software and they might know a little bit about what's going on in the industry. But they're not DOS gurus.

The thing that separates the Weenie from the DOS Weenie is basically effort. A DOS Weenie spends extra time learning why things are done the way they are. Weenies only have memorized how something is done. They see obvious solutions, or borrow

Type of PC	Microprocessor Number
PC, PC/XT & all clones	8088, 8086, V20, V30
PC-AT & all clones	80286
'386 system	80386
'486 system	80486

Figure 1: Shown above are microprocessor numbers for each of the basic PC types.

solutions from others. But DOS Weenie—our guru—comes up with new solutions and innovations.

DOS Weenies are what most of you reading this want to become. The secrets aren't that hidden. It just requires a little more effort than most people are willing to exert. But don't worry; that's what books like this will help you learn.

KNOWLEDGE OF TERMS

Computers are loaded with terms, some new and some perverted variations of things we already know about. There are nouns that become verbs, command names that become adjectives, and those unique verb-noun-adjective combos (like "fax") that dot this industry like pimples on a 14-year-old.

As a DOS guru or future DOS guru, you should be familiar with the following terms that apply to software:

Software/Program/Application

All of these terms refer to software. "Program" is the official term (actually a verb/noun) that refers to the instructions in the software. Program is to software as vehicle is to car.

"Application" is a fancier term for software. It implies activity, that you get something done with the software—software with a purpose. Application is to software as transportation is to car.

Starting/Running/Launching

Start, run, and launch are three interchangeable terms used to describe that actions you take to use a particular piece of software. You start *WordStar*, you run Lotus *1-2-3*, you launch *dBASE*. They all describe the same thing.

Loading

Loading is when you transfer something from disk into memory. For example, you load a worksheet into your spreadsheet application; you load a document into your word processor.

Loading also implies that something has been saved:

Saving

Saving is the process of permanently storing your efforts. You save your database to disk. It's the opposite of loading.

Printing

Printing is important to give you that vital hardcopy, a permanent record of your electronic efforts.

Quitting/Exiting

Once you're done with an application, you'll need to quit, or exit to DOS. This is a step some Total Weenies leave out. Instead of quitting to DOS, they'll whack the reset button or turn the system off and on again.

Wrong!

To finish using software you should always exit properly and return to DOS. From there you can run your other applications, or shut the system down for the day.

The above are the basic terms associated with computer software. There's nothing fancy or secret about anything there. In fact, you should be familiar with them all.

Computer hardware has these terms associated with it:

CPU/Microprocessor/(some number)

Your computer's brain is its CPU, or Central Processing Unit. This chip is also called the "microprocessor" or it's referred to by its chip number. The table on page 6 shows which chip numbers are found in the different types of PC systems.

System Unit

The system unit is the main "box" part of the PC. It contains the disk drives, both hard and floppy, your system's CPU, memory, power supply, expansion cards, and all the internal parts of the system.

Motherboard

The main piece of circuitry in your PC is the motherboard. It's actually a fiberglass sheet that contains the microprocessor, BIOS, ROM, expansion slots, and a slew of electronic goodies resembling some sort of exotic snack dish.

BIOS

BIOS stands for Basic Input/Output System. It consists of computer instructions permanently encoded into your system on a ROM chip. (BIOS is also called ROM.) BIOS contains the basic instructions for dealing with the various parts of your computer. It contains simple interfaces to the printer, display, and keyboard, and provides most of the basics required to write PC software. This is why having a PC-compatible BIOS is important to running DOS software. (DOS operates at a higher level than the BIOS.)

RAM/Memory

One of the most central parts of your computer is its RAM or memory. The amount of work you can get done on your PC is directly proportional to the amount of RAM you have. The more RAM, the faster the work goes and the more your software can do.

RAM has become a major roadblock for PC applications. DOS imposes a 640K limit on the size of your computer's RAM, though some microprocessors can access four-million times that amount. So having RAM and knowing what to do with it is important.

Formatted Capacity	Diskette Size	Comments
360K	5$1/4$-inch	Double sided/double density
720K	3$1/2$-inch	Double sided/double density
1.2 MB	5$1/4$-inch	Double sided/high capacity
1.4 MB	3$1/2$-inch	Double sided/high capacity

Figure 2: The table above lists the PC's four popular diskette formats.

Monitor/Display/Screen

Your computer communicates with you via its monitor, which is connected to a display adapter card inside the system unit. The monitor is often called the display or screen, though these terms seem to apply to the information displayed on the monitor. The monitor itself usually refers to the physical device.

Keyboard

You communicate with your computer via the keyboard. Keyboards on a PC can be maddening. For most, the touch and feel is fine. It's the key placement that drives you nuts. Important keys to locate on a PC keyboard include the backslash key, \, used extensively by DOS, and the ESC key. Hunting down these two little pests can be a hassle on an unfamiliar keyboard.

Peripherals

Anything besides your system unit, monitor and keyboard is considered a peripheral in PC-speak. These include devices you can connect to your computer for a variety of purposes, including the all-important printer.

Other common peripherals include: the computer mouse, modems, plotters, external disk drives, scanners, video digitizers, musical instruments, and scientific monitoring devices (such as joysticks).

There are also general computer terms you should be familiar with, as well: bits, bytes, K, megabytes, boot, as well as standard DOS terms: COPY, FORMAT, ERASE, subdirectory, root directory, and so on.

If any of this is beyond you, consider a good introductory book on DOS. Otherwise, the common ground is established and it's time to work on your guru diploma.

PC STYLES

The standard type of PC is the desktop model, which looks similar to the original PC-AT's case (especially when you squint). But there are other types of PCs: laptops, tower models, portables, and notebook and hand held systems. These are all PCs and most of them work the same as the traditional desktop model, with a few subtle variations.

The only major difference between all the models is in the diskette format. The PC currently sports four different popular types of disk formats, as shown in the table above.

There are two reasons for bringing this up:

Laptop PCs, and some newer systems, use only 3½-inch diskettes. Especially if you work with more than one type of computer, having a common diskette format between them can really help move the data back and forth. The trend shows that the 3½-inch diskette will eventually replace the 5¼-inch models (they're just that much better). Until that happens, there will be compatibility problems.

Two density standards exist; the older 5¼- and 3½-inch diskette formats used a double-density diskette format. Improvements in disk media technology have allowed computers to store much more information on the same-sized diskette. So there's a diskette capacity difference as well as a size difference.

All software is still distributed on the low, 360K- and 720K-capacity diskettes. The higher capacity diskettes only exist on some of the fancier, high-end systems. But still, there are compatibility problems: Low-capacity drives can only read low-capacity diskettes and you can't put a 3½-inch diskette into a 5¼-inch drive no matter how you fold it.

As a common standard for all machines, use the low-density diskettes. But for one machine or personal use, use the high-capacity diskettes (especially for backup or archiving files). That way you should limit your compatibility problems.

HOW TO FIND DOS SECRETS

So far all this information may be review for you. If not, and if you're still interested, you're on the way to becoming a DOS guru. But that still leaves the subject of locating those DOS secrets up in the air.

How does one go about finding DOS secrets?

Just because something is secret doesn't mean it's hidden. Information exists all over the place, but there are two tips I can offer that will help you locate these hidden tricks.

Read the Manual

Some manuals are difficult to follow. But the majority are full of good information about the product. The problem? Manuals aren't written by professional writers who are used to explaining technical concepts in a non-technical way. Instead, they're written by someone at the software development house who is already intimate with the product and doesn't understand a beginner's needs and wishes. Manuals are also restricted in size by the packaging in which the software comes.

The information is there in the manual. Sometimes it pays to work the program for a few weeks and then come back and read the manual. Or, if it exists, you can buy a good book on the subject. But if that still doesn't help, you can try my second tip for becoming a DOS guru.

Fiddle

Fiddling involves doing things with the software that you wouldn't normally do. For example, suppose you open up the manual to the section on "Exporting Data." You have absolutely no need for such a function, but you try it anyway. Lo and behold, you realize that the function is something you can use after all. That's fiddling, and it also lets you become more intimate with your software. (And you paid for that feature, after all.)

Another feature you should fiddle with are macros. Macros really can make life easier. They work by modifying routine tasks you do with your PC and can come in handy in the most unusual of instances. A simple macro, one of my favorites in fact, is one that automatically types my name and address at the end of each letter. Other macros do painful, redundant things over and over. It really makes using the computer easier.

Fiddling also involves trying unusual things. For example, I discovered an unusual command in my backup program the other day. If I press Control-R during the startup screen, it immediately repeats the last backup I did. Since I backup the same files every day, this has proven to be a great time saver. Yet—the Control-R trick isn't in any of the manuals. I only discovered it by fiddling.

Before moving on, I'll admit that most people fear fiddling. They're afraid it will irrevocably damage their system. But this is really hard to do. In fact, the worst that will happen (absolute worse) is that you may need to reset your system. Most software has too many built-in safeguards to prevent you from doing something harmful. (Read the warning messages to be sure!)

SUMMARY

There's nothing hard about being a DOS guru. It all boils down to having the incentive. Once you have that, then other things such as reading the manual and fiddling will come naturally. You should note that this not only applies to DOS, but to learning all software.

Most of the information covered here is basic. There are no secrets. But starting with the next chapter, you'll learn some tricks that have been deeply hidden in the DOS manual for years. Secret stuff. And beneficial.

CHAPTER 2

About DOS

Before you truly can become a DOS guru, you'll have to learn more about DOS than the average computer user. This information isn't required. But then again, no information is "required."

This chapter describes some basics about DOS, some stuff you may already know but good to review. There are three sections:

- How the PC boots
- At the DOS prompt
- Keyboard tricks

There's more to starting a PC than sticking a DOS disk in the drive and flipping the switch. A lot of behind-the-scenes stuff goes on, which may explain to you why some things are done the way they are. After the system boots, you're placed at the familiar DOS prompt. But are you really familiar with it? And finally, there are some keyboard tricks every DOS user should be familiar with.

HOW THE PC BOOTS

There are as many as seven steps that take place when you turn on a computer and boot DOS. Note that these steps only happen if you have a DOS diskette in the floppy drive when you power on, or your hard drive is already configured with DOS.

The seven steps are:

- The bootstrap loader
- The disk's boot sector
- The DOS BIOS & SYSINIT
- The DOS kernel
- CONFIG.SYS
- The command interpreter
- AUTOEXEC.BAT

The Bootstrap Loader

Inside your PC are pre-programmed startup instructions. These instructions are actually part of your BIOS, or ROM, which provides all the low-level interfaces in your computer. (It's DOS that provides the high-level interfaces, primarily between the computer, the disk drives, your software, and you.)

When you first snap on the power switch, the BIOS performs a Power-On Self Test, or POST. The POST checks out all your internal hardware, tests all the memory, and makes sure everything is ready to run. If not, you get a POST error message or your PC beeps at you. If everything's okay, the BIOS scans for a diskette in Drive A or a hard disk, Drive C.

If a disk is found, the bootstrap loader program is run. "Bootstrap" comes from the phrase "being pulled up by your bootstraps." That's a figurative way of explaining how a PC comes on in the morning. With its last dying breath, your BIOS loads the first several bytes of the diskette in Drive A or the hard drive into memory.

The Disk's Boot Sector

The first 512 bytes on a disk are referred to as its *boot sector*. Those bytes are loaded into memory by the BIOS bootstrapper and then executed like a program. If the disk isn't bootable, the program in the boot sector displays a message, such as:

```
Non-System disk or disk error
Replace and strike any key when ready
```

However, if the disk is bootable, the boot sector will begin loading an operating system from the disk. Nearly every computer works this way: With a bootstrap loader in ROM loading in a small segment of disk, and then larger and larger segments. Under DOS, a bootable disk's boot sector will look for and load DOS's BIOS program from the root directory.

The DOS BIOS & SYSINIT

The program the boot sector looks for and loads is called IBMBIO.COM for PC-DOS systems, and IO.SYS for MS-DOS systems. Both files do the same thing: provide low-level interfaces between DOS and the computer's hardware and BIOS.

The DOS BIOS program also initiates a program called SYSINIT, which is part of the IBMBIO.COM or IO.SYS programs. SYSINIT then supervises the remainder of DOS's boot.

The DOS Kernel

One of SYSINIT's first jobs is to load the DOS kernel program. This is the first real part of DOS, also known as the DOS kernel. For PC-DOS the kernel is named IBMDOS.COM; MS-DOS calls it MSDOS.SYS. Both versions contain the core routines which we call DOS. But it's still only the central part, the kernel, of the operating system.

After the kernel program is found and loaded, SYSINIT looks for a file named CONFIG.SYS in your boot disk's root directory.

CONFIG.SYS

CONFIG.SYS is your system's configuration file. It's used to tell DOS a number of things, as well as to load special programs called device drivers.

On the DOS side, CONFIG.SYS allocates memory for DOS to use when dealing with files and disk drives. It also specifies the location of the command interpreter, COMMAND.COM, in most cases.

CONFIG.SYS is also responsible for loading device drivers. These are special programs that build on the foundation of DOS. They let your system interface with unusual hardware, such as a computer mouse or CD-ROM drive, or they control things in your computer such as the display or memory.

CONFIG.SYS is an optional program. If it's not found, SYSINIT will look for COMMAND.COM and execute it. And if COMMAND.COM isn't found, then you'll get a "Bad or missing command interpreter" message and the computer will freeze.

The Command Interpreter

SYSINIT's final job is to load a command interpreter. The command interpreter is your interface with DOS. Normally, it's COMMAND.COM. However, a different interpreter can be specified via CONFIG.SYS (it's covered in Chapter Seven).

When you use DOS, it's the command interpreter you see. COMMAND.COM supplies the ugly C prompt, where you enter all DOS's cryptic commands.

But after COMMAND.COM is run, it looks for the final set of the DOS boot process: the AUTOEXEC.BAT program.

Function	PC-DOS	MS-DOS
DOS BIOS	IBMBIO.COM	IO.SYS
DOS KERNEL	IBMDOS.COM	MSDOS.SYS
Command Interpreter	COMMAND.COM	COMMAND.COM

Figure 3: *The table above lists DOS's boot programs between PC-DOS and MS-DOS.*

AUTOEXEC.BAT

AUTOEXEC.BAT is a batch file, a special type of text file that contains DOS commands. (Batch files are covered in Chapter Five.) COMMAND.COM will always look for AUTOEXEC.BAT in your boot disk's root directory and, if found, will execute any commands you have stored there. Otherwise, DOS will ask you to enter the date and time, then display its startup message and you'll be at the DOS prompt, ready to type commands.

More information on AUTOEXEC.BAT, and how useful it can be, is covered in Chapter Seven.

AT THE DOS PROMPT

The DOS prompt is where you get all your work done in DOS. It's also referred to as the command line or command prompt.

Normally, the DOS prompt consists of the letter of the current drive and a greater-than sign:

C>

However, using the PROMPT command, you can customize the prompt to just about anything. And if you use the ANSI.SYS screen driver, you can add all sorts of unusual effects and color to a command prompt. (Those secrets are covered in later chapters.)

To use the command prompt, you simply enter a DOS command or the name of a program. DOS then interprets your input and carries out your instructions (you hope). Ergo, the "command interpreter."

The command line interface, which is how DOS gives you access to its features, isn't the best way to run a computer. Many people think a better approach is to use a graphic shell or text-based menu system.

Several applications are available that give you fancier ways of interfacing with a computer. Microsoft *Windows* is the IBM- and Microsoft-approved way of using a DOS computer in the future. Other applications give you powerful menus that allow you to work the computer and run your software by pressing only a few keys. But these applications all work on top of the basic DOS described in this book.

Though graphic shells and menu systems are easier for most people, especially in large organizations, to use, they're not DOS. You should always know a little DOS, just like you should know basic mechanical things like using a screwdriver, changing a light bulb, or changing your car's tires. As a future guru, you should know about the shells and menus, but concentrate on mastering DOS first. And you can start mastering DOS by learning one thing few people know about when they use DOS's command prompt: the editing keys.

The Editing Keys

At the DOS prompt you can enter and edit DOS commands. All characters you type, up to 128, are displayed on the keyboard. Note that the 128 value includes the final ENTER keystroke.

Key	Symbol	Function
ENTER	↵	Accept line
Backspace	⇐	Erase character to the left
Left arrow	←	Erase character to the left
ESC	^[	Erase line and start over
Control-C	^C	Cancel input, reset prompt

Figure 4: Shown above are the standard keystrokes used to edit the command line.

The following keystrokes are used to edit your command line. Backspace and the left arrow are used to erase the previous character. Pressing ESC erases the whole line, moving the cursor back to the DOS prompt. Note that when you do so, the line isn't erased. Instead, the backslash (\) character is displayed and the cursor moves down to the next line. This is the same as canceling the line and starting over.

Finally, if you want to cancel input, you can press Control-C. When you do, ^C will be displayed and another DOS prompt will appear. Note that pressing Control-Break will do the same thing.

In addition to those keys, DOS uses the function keys to help you edit the command line. Many people don't figure this out and lose some of the benefits the function keys give you.

The secret to understanding how these function keys work is knowing that DOS keeps all the keystrokes you enter at the command prompt in a *template*.

All the characters you type are copied into the template. It's DOS's way of giving you primitive editing functions. So instead of retyping a command, you can simply edit the DOS command line or re-use the template. Yes, it's true: you can edit the DOS command line. But the functions are so primitive that few people really bother to learn them.

Key	Function
F1 or →	Move right one character in the template
F2	Display all characters in the template up to the indicated character
F3	Display remaining characters in the template
F4	Delete all characters in the template up to the indicated character
F5	Reset the template
F6 or ^Z	Display the end-of-file marker (used for creating files from the keyboard)
F7	Display the null character, ^@

Figure 5: *Shown above is a list of the function keys and which editing commands they perform.*

To test how these keys work, type in the following. Note that I'm using C:\ as the DOS prompt, though yours may look different.

At the command prompt type "this is a test" but don't press ENTER:

```
C:\) this is a test
```

You could press Control-C, ESC or ENTER right now to test those keys. But forget ENTER: you'll doubtless get an error message. Instead, press F5. This resets the template by emptying its contents and replacing them with whatever you've entered so far. You should see:

```
C:\) this is a test@
```

Note that the cursor will be displayed on the next line down, right below the first "T." You can now edit the line. To see how F1 works, press it six times. You will see:

```
C:\) this is a test@
     this i
```

The right arrow key does the same thing; press it three times:

```
C:\) this is a test@
     this is a
```

The Backspace and right arrow keys move you backward in the template—but they don't erase characters. Type Backspace or the right arrow key until the line is erased (but it's not gone—it's still in the template):

You can edit in the template by retyping commands. For example, type "That" and then the right arrow key to the end of the line.

```
C:\) this is a test@
     that is a test
```

You've edited the template. But you haven't changed it. Only by pressing F5 (or ENTER) will changes be written to the template. To prove it, press left arrow to the start of the line, then F1 or right arrow to re-display the template. "this" is still there.

The DEL and INS keys on the keyboard can be used to delete and insert text into the template. But you're working "blind" because you can't really see what you're deleting. For example, these instructions tell you how to insert "not" into the template, and how to use the F2, search command:

- Press F2. The next character you type is a search character. Every character in the template up to that character will be displayed. So to search to the "a", type "a" after F2:

```
C:\) this is a test@
     this is
```

- To insert "not," press the INS key once and type "not" followed by a space:

```
C:\) this is a test@
     this is not
```

- To display the rest of the template, press F3:

```
C:\) this is a test@
     this is not a test,
```

The DEL key deletes keys from the template, but again you can't see them. Pressing F3 will display the remainder of the keyboard, and you can always backspace over anything to recover the template's original contents.

Did you notice how F3 displays the rest of the template? That's a handy DOS tip for you: Pressing F3 at the command line always re-displays your last-entered command.

F4 is used like F2, but instead of displaying all characters it deletes all characters up to the one you enter. So to quickly delete not from the examples, do the following:

- Press F5 to copy the new text into the template:

```
C:\) this is a test@
     this is not a test@
```

■ Press F2 then "n" to search up to the "n" in "not":

```
C:\> this is a test@
     this is not a test@
     this is
```

■ Press F4 and then "a" to delete all characters in the template up to the "a." (Or you could press the DEL key four times.

■ Press F3 to display the rest of the line:

```
C:\> this is a test@
     this is not a test@
     this is a test
```

The DOS editing keys can be used in any program that supports a similar, crummy interface. For example, the horrid DOS text editor, EDLIN (which hasn't changed in four releases of DOS), uses the same function/editing keys. A few programs that support DOS-like input will use them as well.

The easiest one to remember is F3. Most people don't bother with the others because you're editing a template you can't see. It's just too hard to know what you're doing. And for a computer that's supposed to make life easier, that's too much to ask for.

KEYBOARD TRICKS

While on the subject of keyboard tricks, the following are other key commands and combinations you can try at the DOS prompt. Some of these will even work in other programs (though not every program will support them). Try them in a few to find out.

Keyboard State Keys

There are three common keyboard state keys:

■ Caps lock
■ Num lock
■ Scroll lock

Caps Lock works like the shift lock on a typewriter keyboard. However, unlike shift lock, only the alphabet keys are switched to UPPER CASE. All other keys on the keyboard, the punctuation and number keys, remain unshifted.

Num Lock is used to transform your keyboard's numeric keypad into a numeric keypad. Normally, the keypad is used for its arrow keys, and Home, Pg Up (page up), etc. Note that some of the newer keyboards have both arrow keys and a numeric keypad, but you still need to have Num Lock ON to use the numbers.

The Scroll Lock key is a real mystery. Only a handful of applications may use it, and then each for a different purpose. Scroll Lock has its roots in some older computer terminals. It's ignored by perhaps 99 percent of PC programs—and DOS.

Other Fun Keys

The Print Screen key is used to send a copy of the text on your screen to your printer. If your printer can display the IBM PC graphic character set, then you'll get those characters printed as well (otherwise the results could be unpredictable).

Print Screen, or "Print Scrn" or "PrtSc," comes in handy to get a quick hardcopy of the information on your screen. But it can be a pain. Accidentally pressing Print Screen when a printer isn't connected to your PC could crash the system (or leave you desperately searching for a printer so that you can keep working). If you're already printing something and you press Print Screen, the results can be garbled.

Some programs turn Print Screen off (which can be done). But in DOS, Print Screen works as advertised, and comes in handy sometimes.

A real "fun" key is the Fn key found on some laptops. Fn stands for function or alternative function. It's usually used in combination with other standard keys that have a dual purpose. For example, a laptop's keyboard may be too small to have an F11 or

F12 key. However, pressing Fn-F9 produces F11 and Fn-F10 produces F12.

The Fn key is color-coded with other keys on the keyboard. That way, you can have access to a desktop PC's wealth of keys without actually having the keys on the keyboard.

CONTROL KEY COMBOS

There are several control-key combinations you can use for various things at the DOS prompt. Some of these may be familiar to you, others may be yet-more-secret DOS treasures:

Control-C or Control-Break

Pressing Control-C or Control-Break at the DOS prompt cancels any DOS command or stops a DOS process, and returns you to the command prompt. If you have the BREAK command set to ON, such as:

```
BREAK ON
```

Then Control-C or Control-Break may also stop some of your applications, also returning you to the command prompt. (BREAK ON or BREAK OFF can be set or reset in CONFIG.SYS or at the command prompt.)

Note that Control-Break is the more powerful of the two, actually triggering a PC "interrupt" that overrides other things going on in the computer. Control-Break will also reset your disk system. If you've ever experienced a scrambled directory when switching floppy diskettes, pressing Control-Break after removing a diskette will solve the problem.

Control-S or Pause

Pressing Control-S is used to pause DOS, typically during a scrolling display of text or other information. You press any key— including Control-S—to continue the display.

The Pause key is similar to Control-S, but it's more powerful. If your keyboard has a Pause key, then pressing it will stop virtually anything and keep the computer in a pensive, waiting state. Pressing any key (other than Pause again) will relieve the computer from its paused state. (Most people press ENTER after pressing Pause.)

Control-P or Control-Print Screen

The Control-P toggle is used to turn DOS's echo-to-printer function on or off. Control-Print Screen also works on some systems. Note that a toggle is an on/off state controlled by one switch: You press Control-P once to turn the function on, then pressing it again will turn it off.

After pressing Control-P, all text you see on the screen will be echoed to the printer. Only by pressing Control-P a second time will the echo-to-printer function be turned off.

Control-P really comes in handy sometimes, yet few people know about it.

THE ALT-KEYPAD TRICK

The PC has over 255 characters in its display repertoire. Yet only the first 127 are capable of being produced directly by the keyboard: The majority of those keys are the upper- and lower-case alphabet, plus the numbers, punctuation keys, and other symbols. Thirty-three "control-characters" can be produced by pressing certain keys in combination with the Control key (these are illustrated in Appendix A).

The upper 128 characters consist of foreign-language character sets, and graphic and mathematical symbols. These characters are referred to as the PC's *extended ASCII* character set. You can't readily produce these characters on the keyboard, but you can display them if you know their number code.

A list of the extended ASCII characters and their number codes is shown in Appendix A. To produce them, or any character (providing you know its code), you can use what I call the Alt-keypad trick.

To produce any of the 255 characters the PC can display, hold the Alt key and type the character's number on the keypad. You must use the keypad. And you must hold down the Alt key until you've entered the entire number. Upon releasing the Alt key, the character corresponding to that number will be displayed.

For example, to enter the á character, which has a code value of 160, do the following:

1. Press and hold the Alt key
2. Type 1 then 6 then 0 on the keypad
3. Release the Alt key

Voilá, you have the á character!

These characters can be used in applications to create graphics, mathematical symbols, or to add foreign language characters to your text (though not all printers will print the characters). In DOS, they can be used to create fancy menus for batch files, or to give files unusual names (which is covered in Chapter Four).

SUMMARY

This has been a general, get-to-know-DOS-better chapter. Actually, there are two subjects covered here: How DOS boots, and keyboard tricks.

DOS does several things when it boots, but important to you are the roles that CONFIG.SYS and AUTOEXEC.BAT play. Why? Because these are two files over which you have direct control. And how you play your CONFIG.SYS and AUTOEXEC.BAT cards will affect how efficiently your PC operates.

Keyboard tricks could have been a separate chapter by itself. DOS has a lot of "secret" little things you can do with the keyboard, from editing the command line using the function keys to echoing DOS to a printer (which beats pressing Print Screen every 25 lines).

The next chapter continues on the same subject of DOS Basics for Gurus with a discussion of devices; a central concept to getting the most from your operating system.

PART TWO

CHAPTER 3

Drives and Devices

Central to knowing DOS is understanding the concept of drives and devices. DOS treats everything in the computer as a device. As such, communications between various devices is possible. This has benefits as far as manipulating files and information in ways you probably never knew were possible.

The subject of DOS and devices is covered in these sections:

- Everything is a device
- Communications between devices
- I/O redirection
- Filters
- The pipe

It's true, everything in DOS is a device. Even the title of this chapter is misleading because a drive is a device. (It's like titling a chapter "Broccoli and Vegetables.")

EVERYTHING IS A DEVICE

DOS communicates with each part of the PC by treating them all the same. It treats the disk drives as a device. Your printer is a device, the serial port is a device, and the screen and keyboards are devices. Everything is a device.

Device Name	Device
AUX	First serial port
CAS	Cassette port (IBM PC-1 only)
CLOCK$	System clock (internal use only!)
COM1	First serial port
COM2	Second serial port
COM3	Third serial port
COM4	Fourth serial port
CON	Console, display and keyboard
LPT1	First printer port
LPT2	Second printer port
LPT3	Third printer port
NUL	"Null," or empty device
PRN	First printer port

Figure 6: Shown above is a chart listing DOS devices and their names.

In addition to these devices, the disk drives are also given device names. The first drive is A:, the second is B:, the first hard drive is C:. Drive device names go all the way up to Z:.

So what's the point?

It all has to deal with information and input/output. DOS treats all devices equally. The way to visualize this is to think of each device (listed in the table) as a disk drive.

The disk drive is the basic device that DOS deals with. Yet, because DOS is device-oriented, it can treat other devices just like a disk drive. The exception is that the disk device is the only one that allows information to be stored in the form of files. But just as you can between disk drives, you can move information—copy files—between DOS devices.

Before moving on, note that some devices are capable of only input or output. A disk drive is capable of both, meaning you can both send and receive information to and from a disk drive. The printer, on the other hand, is an output-only device. You can only send information to the printer; none is ever returned.

The CON device represents both your keyboard and screen. In this instance, when input is requested from CON it comes from the keyboard. When output is sent to CON, it's shown on the screen.

A weirdo type of device is the NUL device. It's an empty hole, nothing really, used primarily to test certain commands, or when a device is required for a command but none is available. (An example is coming up.)

COMMUNICATIONS BETWEEN DEVICES

Some computer operating systems are built to deal with disk drives as independent units. They understand that you can copy information (in the form of files) between two disk drives, or between different locations on the same disk. But since they only deal with the drives as devices, special programs must be written to move information from a disk drive to other parts of the computer, such as the printer or display.

In DOS, everything is a device. So just as you would use the COPY command to copy a file from one drive to another, you can use COPY to copy a file from one device to another. Since DOS treats all parts of the computer as a device, this is possible.

Copying Between Devices

For example, your AUTOEXEC.BAT or CONFIG.SYS file is a text file. This means its contents are readable, composed of text as opposed to data and program files, which the computer and your software can read but you can't.

To see the contents of your AUTOEXEC.BAT file, you use the TYPE command at the DOS prompt:

```
TYPE AUTOEXEC.BAT
```

This causes the contents of your AUTOEXEC.BAT file to be displayed on the screen. But isn't the screen a device? It's the CON device, for console. The screen is the output part of the CON device. So what would happen if you used the COPY command to copy AUTOEXEC.BAT to the CON device?

Type the following, but don't press ENTER yet:

```
COPY AUTOEXEC.BAT CON
```

This reads "Copy the information in the file AUTOEXEC.BAT to the CON device." CON is used here just like the name of a disk drive or file. Will it work? Yes, because DOS treats everything like a device. What does it do? Press ENTER.

The COPY command copies AUTOEXEC.BAT to your screen—the same as TYPE did. The only difference is you'll see "1 File(s) copied" after the listing.

Copying to the Printer

The most common use of devices with the COPY command is to send output to your printer.

The PRN device is used to represent the first printer in your system, the standard printer. It could also be LPT1, or if you're using a serial printer, it could be COM1. (Only if you've re-assigned the COM1 printer to LPT1 will the PRN device represent it. This is covered in Chapter Seven.)

To get a hardcopy of your AUTOEXEC.BAT file, simply copy its contents to the printer:

```
COPY AUTOEXEC.BAT PRN
```

This reads, "Copy the AUTOEXEC.BAT file to the PRN (printer) device." Your printer should be on before you do this. Also, note that the paper won't eject from the printer. (Press the Form Feed button on the printer to spit it out.) The "1 File(s) copied" message is still displayed on the CON device.

This is really the only way to print text files in DOS. DOS has a PRINT command, but that loads a really cheap form of print spooler and shouldn't be used.

Copying at the Console

The input part of the CON device is supplied by the keyboard. So if you specify CON as the first argument of the COPY command, the information will be coming from the keyboard, as opposed to a file on disk in the previous examples.

For example, type the following, but don't press ENTER:

```
COPY CON TEST
```

This reads, "Copy information from the CON (console, keyboard) device to a file on disk named TEST." If TEST doesn't exist, the COPY command will create it—just as it would create any file when you use COPY. The difference here is that the information is coming from the CONsole, your keyboard, instead of a file on disk.

Press ENTER.

You'll see the cursor drop down to the next line, where it will blink humbly. It's waiting for you, master of the CON device, to start entering characters. Go ahead, start typing away.

As you type, you can use DOS's function/editing keys to correct any mistakes. Remember you can only enter up to 128 characters on a line. So press ENTER at the end of a line, as opposed to the end of a paragraph as you would in a word processor. Also, because this is the "DOS editor" you're using, you can't press the up arrow key to correct a line.

If your mind is dry, type the following:

```
Roses are red,
Violets are blue,
Sugar is sweet
And M&Ms are round.
```

When you're done, you need to signal the COPY command that your "file" is at its end. To do this, you need to produce a Control-Z, DOS's end-of-file character. You make a Control-Z by typing Control-Z or by pressing the F6 key (which does the same thing). You'll see the following displayed on your screen:

```
^Z
```

Press ENTER to send it to the COPY command. Then you'll see the "1 File(s) copied" message, meaning your file has been created. (Use TYPE or COPY the file to the CON device to see your creation.)

A nickname for this file-creating technique is COPY CON. You're using the COPY command to create a file via the CON device. It's a quick and dirty method of making little text files, but not very efficient for larger files. For that, you might as well use a text editor or word processor.

Note that you must specify a filename when copying to the disk drive device. You can't type "COPY CON A:". By definition, the disk drive device requires a filename or you'll get an error.

The DOS Typewriter

Aside from copying to a file, you can copy from the CON device to other devices as well. One of the most practical is the printer device.

```
COPY CON PRN
```

This command causes COPY to link your CON device, the keyboard, with the PRN device, your printer. While it's not as smooth as a typewriter, or as cheap, it does work—a line at a time.

After entering the above command, type a few lines of text. Notice that each line only appears on the printer after you press ENTER. (Some printers may not print until their internal buffer is full. If so, keep typing away.)

When you get to the bottom of the page, type a Control-L. Control-L is the "form feed" character, and when sent to any DOS printer it causes the current page to be ejected and the next page to line up.

When you're done (or fed up) with the typewriter mode, press Control-Z or F6 to turn it off. Remember to press that final ENTER to send the ^Z to the COPY command and return you to the DOS prompt.

I/O REDIRECTION

I/O redirection is a cryptic name for sending information around inside a computer. The theme here is still devices and moving information. But by using I/O redirection, you can shuffle off information from its normal destination and route it elsewhere.

DOS uses what are called "standard devices" for certain chores. The standard input device is your keyboard. The standard output device is the screen. These devices are used all the time you use DOS. For example, when you use the TYPE command, it automatically sends its output to the screen—the standard output device. When you work in a DOS program, such as EDLIN or DEBUG, it automatically expects its input from the standard input device, the keyboard.

But these things can change.

Using I/O redirection, you can specify a device other than the screen or keyboard as the standard input or output device. You can't make the changes permanent, but for most instances, a quick redirection really helps when you need information manipulated.

There are two symbols used to I/O redirection: ⟨, the less-than, and, ⟩ the greater-than. The symbol is used to redirect input, meaning input will be provided by a device other than the console. The symbol redirects output, sending the output to a device other than the console.

Input redirection using ⟨ is a tricky thing. There are only a few examples that are safe to use. Why? Because while input redirection is active, your keyboard is dead. If the input provided from another device is faulty, your computer will hang. Because of this, the only true example of input redirection is covered later in this book, in Chapter Nine.

Output redirection is more popular, and it has many uses.

Output Redirection

Most DOS commands display their results on the screen. Why? Because they use the standard output device. But this can be changed via output redirection.

For example, when you type the DIR command, you see a listing of the files on the screen:

```
C:\>DIR
 Volume in drive C is TOO LOUD
 Directory of C:\
GRAPHICS    ⟨DIR⟩      9-25-88    11:26a
DOS         ⟨DIR⟩      9-24-88    12:49a
WP          ⟨DIR⟩      9-24-88     4:26p
AUTOEXEC BAT   1102    3-16-90     4:04p
COMMAND COM   26268    2-20-89    12:00p
CONFIG SYS      185    3-19-90     3:28p
    6 File(s) 14485120 bytes free
```

But you can redirect the DIR command's output to another device by specifying that device after the ⟩ symbol. Type the following but don't press ENTER:

```
DIR ⟩ FILE
```

This tells DOS to "Display the contents of the current directory, but redirect the output to a file FILE." If FILE doesn't exist, it will be created. If it does exist, it will be overwritten. Press ENTER.

Nothing much happens. But if you examine the directory again, you'll see a new file FILE. Examining that file will reveal the output of the DIR command.

You can also get a hardcopy of your directory listing by specifying the PRN device:

```
DIR > PRN
```

This redirects the output of the DIR command to the printer. It's much better than pressing Print Screen every few lines, and it's much more reliable than the Control-P toggle.

You may notice that your directory listing is still in the printer. To eject the page you can lean over and press the Form Feed button. Or you can send the Form Feed character, Control-L, directly to the printer. How? With more I/O redirection. Type the following:

```
ECHO ^L > PRN
```

To produce ^L, type Control-L, the form feed character.

Normally, the ECHO command displays any following text on the screen, the standard output device. But if you change the standard output device, it will echo the text to another device, in this case the printer.

Here's another trick:

Type the following at the command prompt:

```
CLS > ZAP
```

This redirects the output of the CLS command, which clears the screen, to a file named ZAP. Since CLS's output has been redirected, your screen won't clear. But a new file named ZAP will appear in your directory. What's in ZAP? Why note use the TYPE command to find out?

```
TYPE ZAP
```

Poof! Your screen is cleared. Can you figure out how that happened?

Appending

Sometimes you'll want to redirect output to a file, but not erase the original contents of the file. In that case, you can use the output redirection with append feature. The symbol is ⟩⟩, double greater than signs.

For example, suppose you want to create a file on disk that contains all the files on disk. To do so, you can move to each subdirectory on your drive and type the following:

```
DIR ⟩⟩ C:\DIRFILE
```

This reads, "Display a directory of the current drive, but redirect the output to a file named DIRFILE in the root directory of Drive C." If DIRFILE doesn't exist, it will be created. If it exists, then the output of the DIR will be appended to the end of the file.

Note that this technique only works with text files. You can't append to the end of a word processing document or worksheet. Sure, it will work. But the results will be far from what you want.

Also, you can use ⟩⟩ with devices besides disk drives. But it's rather silly. "Appending" to the printer doesn't make sense.

FILTERS

Moving information between devices has a lot of applications. But there are times when you want the information modified along the way. In those instances, you can insert what DOS calls a "filter" between the device producing the input and the destination of the output.

DOS comes with three filter programs:

- MORE
- SORT
- FIND

Each one of these can be used to modify the output of a DOS command, or to filter text manipulated by I/O redirection.

The MORE Filter

The MORE filter is used to pause long displays of text. Normally, when you TYPE a long file, the text whizzes past you before you get a chance to read it all. You can try pressing Control-S or Pause, but that's really inefficient—especially when you remember that computers are supposed to make life easier for you.

The MORE filter causes the words "more" to be displayed after every 24th line of text. It then pauses the display and waits for you to press a key before the next screen of text is shown.

MORE, like all filters, requires both input and output to work. In this case the input comes from a file. The output is usually the standard output device. For example:

```
MORE < TEXTFILE
```

MORE receives its input here from the text file TEXTFILE on disk. It will display the contents of that file one screen at a time, each time pausing to display "more" and waiting for you to press a key.

Some people get confused with MORE, and other filters, because they don't supply any arguments. They will type MORE at the command prompt, press ENTER, and expect something exciting to happen. But nothing does. Why? Because MORE is expecting input from the standard input device—your keyboard. You must specify a file as the input for the MORE filter to work properly.

The SORT Filter

The SORT filter modifies information in the same format as MORE. But the result is much different. SORT's job is to alphabetically sort all the lines in a file. So it has some nifty uses to sort your directory listings (which are covered in Chapter Four).

   To see SORT in action create a text file on disk with items to
sort. To do this, type the following at the DOS command prompt:

```
COPY CON FRUIT
```

   After pressing ENTER, type the names of some fruits, one on
each line:

```
APPLE
BANANA
ORANGE
GRAPE
KIWI
GUAVA
```

On the last line type Control-Z and ENTER to end the file.
To sort this file, use the SORT filter as follows:

```
SORT 〈 FRUIT
```

   You'll then see a sorted list of your fruit on the display. But
what if you want to save that list in a file? Then you can use output
redirection as follows:

```
SORT 〈FRUIT〉 SFRUIT
```

   Here, the output of the SORT command will be redirected to
the file SFRUIT (which will be created) on disk. Note how output
redirection with the SORT filter makes sense, whereas output
redirection of MORE does not.

   Also, you can use the SORT command to sort items "on the
fly." Just type SORT on the command line by itself, followed by
the items you want sorted:

```
SORT
APPLE
BANANA
ORANGE
GRAPE
KIWI
GUAVA
```

Press Control-Z and you'll see the sorted listed displayed. Or you could have originally entered:

```
SORT 〉 FRUIT
```

This would cause whatever you typed at the console to be saved to the file FRUIT on disk—and in a sorted format.

SORT has two optional switches which can help control the order and type of sort being performed. You can specify a switch after SORT to manipulate the sorted order of items produced by SORT's output.

The /R switch is used to reverse the order of the sort. If you typed:

```
SORT /R〉 FRUIT
```

The FRUIT file created on disk would contain a Z to A listing of sorted fruit.

The /+*n* switch is used to force SORT to sort on column *n* of the file, as opposed to the first column. For example, if you're sorting a table of information in a file, and you want to sort on column 14, you'd enter:

```
SORT /+14 〈TABLE〉 STABLE
```

This would sort the information in the file TABLE on column 14, and then send the sorted output to the file STABLE.

The FIND Filter

FIND is the lamest of the filter programs DOS provides. It's used to display the lines in a file that contain a matching string of text. For example:

```
FIND "My brain" FILE1 FILE2 FILE3
```

This command, which doesn't use I/O redirection at all, will search for the text string "My brain" in the three files FILE1, FILE2, and FILE3. If found, the name of the file and the lines in the file where the text was found would be displayed.

There are better utilities for locating text in lost files than FIND, and they're faster too. One of the best is called GREP, and it's available in the public domain, from computer clubs, on-line networks, or software warehouses.

THE PIPE

A distant cousin to 〈 and 〉 is the pipe symbol, I, the vertical bar. Called the pipe, it's used to translate the standard output of a DOS command into the standard input needed for a filter.

DOS commands that display information send it to the standard output device. For example, when you using the TYPE command to view the contents of a text file, you enter a command like:

```
TYPE TEXTFILE
```

TEXTFILE is then displayed on the screen. But what if you wanted to use the MORE filter? The file is longer than one screen and you want it to pause every screen full of text. Consider:

```
TYPE TEXTFILE 〉 MORE
```

This would appear to redirect the output of the TYPE TEXTFILE command into the MORE filter. But it doesn't work that way. Instead, you'll be sending the output of the TYPE command to a file on disk called "MORE." Output redirection sends the output of a command to another device—not through a filter.

In order to pipe the output of a DOS command through a filter, you need a pipe.

The pipe, I, is placed after the DOS command that produces output. It then pipes that output into the filter as standard input. For example:

```
TYPE TEXTFILE | MORE
```

Here, the output of the TYPE TEXTFILE command is piped into the MORE filter as input. This has the desired effect, displaying TEXTFILE (or whatever file you specify) one screen at a time.

Using the Pipe With DIR

Most often, you'll be using the pipe with the DIR command. The pipe is used to convert DIR's output into input for a filter, most notable the SORT filter. This way you can produce a variety of sorted directory listings.

To sort a directory alphabetically, type:

```
DIR | SORT
```

You may see something like the following displayed:

```
 6 File(s) 14485120 bytes free
 Directory of C:\
 Volume in drive C is TOO LOUD
AUTOEXEC BAT  1102   3-16-90    4:04p
COMMAND COM  26268   2-20-89   12:00p
CONFIG SYS     185   3-19-90    3:28p
DOS        ⟨DIR⟩     9-24-88   12:49a
GRAPHICS   ⟨DIR⟩     9-25-88   11:26a
WP         ⟨DIR⟩     9-24-88    4:26p
```

Why does it look so funky? Because the extra text, information about the drive and files, is also displayed. And occasionally you may see some oddly named files in there as well. They're special temporary files created by the SORT command. Note that they're deleted after SORT is done.

You can use SORT with its optional switches to sort the directory in different orders. Note that the files in the directory listing are all evenly formatted. So to sort based on file size, you only need specify that column offset. The same applies to sort on the date or time, simply specify the offset next to the SORT command's /+ option.

The following table shows the variations of the SORT command when used with DIR and the pipe:

DIR/SORT command	Sorts files by...
DIR I SORT /+10	Filename extension
DIR I SORT /+14	Size in bytes
DIR I SORT /+25	Creation date
DIR I SORT /+35	Creation time

Figure 7: Shown above are the options for SORT when sorting a directory.

The key thing to remember about the pipe is that it takes the output of a DOS command and supplies it as input for a filter. Otherwise, you can use simple I/O redirection to give a filter its input.

SUMMARY

This chapter dealt with devices which, as it turns out, is a big part of DOS. Rather than limit DOS to manipulating information via files on disk drives, you can send information between any of DOS's devices, you can redirect input and output, and you can use filters to modify the output.

The next chapter covers another large part of DOS, file organization. It's yet another area, like devices, that the DOS manual is rather weak on explaining. And there are even more tricks and secrets to uncover.

CHAPTER 4

File Organization

The year 1983 saw the introduction of the IBM PC/XT and DOS 2.0. Thus was ushered in the era of hard disks on DOS computers. The PC's hardware can handle the hard disk. And the software, using the improvements to DOS in version 2, could handle a hard drive. But can the user?

This chapter deals with the problems of file organization, or how to manage a lot of information (files) in a big space (your hard drive). Even if you don't have a hard drive (and you should), there are things to learn here.

Though the subject is vast and the territory wild, the subject here can successfully be managed in four sections:

- Files and filenames
- Working with subdirectories
- Building a working structure
- General hard disk management

Filenames and pathnames provide the basis for dealing with information on your hard drive. The rest of it, primarily organization using subdirectories, is unexplored territory. DOS makes no rule about how you organize your system. That's all up to you. Now isn't that a scary thought?

FILES AND FILENAMES

The file is the basic unit of information on your hard drive. There are three different types of files:

- Program files
- Text files
- Data files

Program files contain programming instructions for the computer. They're software, applications that you can run to do something or to help you control the computer.

Text files are unique because they contain readable text. Also called ASCII files, the information in these files can by TYPEd at in DOS and the contents don't look like Greek.

Data files aren't program files in that they don't (usually) contain software. But unlike text files, the contents of a data file are intended for some application to read and manipulate. They could contain programming code, in the form of an "overlay" file, or they could contain text—but in a special word processing document format, not readily understood by a human.

The only distinction DOS makes between any of these three file types is by its name, specifically the filename extension.

Program files under DOS have one of three filename extensions:

.COM
.EXE
.BAT

COM and EXE files contain executable program code. The COM format is the oldest, borrowed from an earlier operating system, CP/M. While COM programs are the fasted to load, they're limited in size to under 64K. The EXE format has no size limit, but they're a little clunkier to load. Presently, with today's memory-hungry applications, EXE programs are most common.

The BAT extension identifies a BATch file. Batch files are really text files, but the text they contain is in the form of special DOS commands. Batch files are covered in Chapter Five.

The purpose of this diatribe is to show you DOS's only rules about what a file is named. COM, EXE, and BAT are the only ways DOS has to know that a file is a program. You can name a file anything else and DOS won't have a clue as to its contents. This problem is compounded when you consider the limitations DOS puts on naming a file.

Naming a File

All information on disk is stored in files, and files are identified by their names. Under DOS, the name uses the 8-dot-3 convention: An eight-letter filename, followed by an optional period and three-letter filename extension.

The name is the primary means of telling what's in a file. And with only eight letters, this limits your creativity a bit. The extension is often used (though not required) to identify the type of file. This stems from the basic COM, EXE and BAT extensions DOS uses. In addition, DOS uses SYS to identify device drivers and BAS for BASIC programs.

Over the years, other extensions have become more-or-less standards when naming DOS files. The most frequently used are: TXT, which means a text file; DOC for a word processing document; DBF for a database file; WKS for a worksheet; and so on. Many applications have their own conventions. And there are many other combinations, as well. But it's not very descriptive.

When naming a file, these are the rules:

■ The filename can be up from one to eight letters long.

■ An optional extension from one to three letters can be specified, and if so it must follow a period after the filename.

■ The filename can consist of all but the following characters: ." /\[ ] : * | ⟨⟩ + = ; , ?

You can add to those 16 characters all the Control-key characters, Control-@ through the space character.

Note that the period is a restricted character, only used to separate the filename from the extension. Also, you can start a filename with any valid filename character. This includes numbers or symbols. A few people believe that you can't start a filename with a number. This isn't true.

But what most people never latch on to is the incredible variety of naming conventions DOS will let you use. Granted, 8-dot-3 isn't much. But you have 181 characters you can use in those 11 positions. That's 256 minus the 16 restricted characters, the 33 Control-key combinations, and 26 lower-case letters, which are converted to upper case when you save the file. (See Appendix A.) That leaves room for a lot of variety.

Secret Naming Tricks

Most people name files using the basic 53-or-so keys accessible from the keyboard. (Remember, lower-case characters are converted to upper case when you save.) Even with those limited characters, people can use the underscore or hyphen in a file to make it more understandable.

For example:

```
TABLE_3.1
```

Here is a valid filename for Table 3.1 in a book. The underscore is used as a separator. Traditionally this is done in programming languages that won't allow for embedded spaces in variable names. It can be done in DOS to put some breathing room between filenames.

```
TABLE-3.1
```

The same is done here with the hyphen. Note how the period and extension are used to identify the number "3.1"? This is valid, but not practical. It's often better to link similar files by their filename extension. So if you were being really clever, and wanted to be able to manipulate all the "tables" in your directory, you could give them similar extensions. Such as:

`.TBL`

Then the files could be named:

```
3-1.TBL
3-2.TBL
3-3.TBL
4-1.TBL
```

This way, you could use the *.TBL (see the following section on wildcards) wildcard to manipulate the whole group at once, either with COPY or some other DOS command.

But beyond these basic characters are the 128 Extended ASCII characters, also valid for naming a file. A complete list of characters is shown in Appendix A. And remember, though they aren't available on the keyboard, you can produce them using the Alt-keypad trick (see Chapter Two).

For example, how's this for a filename:

`MY INFO.DOC`

Looks wrong, doesn't it? A space is an invalid character. If you tried to access the above file, DOS would think you just mean "MY" and ignore the rest of the line as garbage. But is that really a space character?

Character 255 in the Extended ASCII set is also a space, though it's called "blank" just to be different. You can produce it at the DOS prompt by typing Alt-2-5-5 (keep the Alt key down while you type 2, 5, 5 on the keypad—release the Alt key.)

How about this for a filename:

μαστηξα.DBF

Looks Greek to me. But if it's a database file containing your favorite brands of chewing gum, then it would make sense to you.

Other oddball combinations are also possible. There's a lot of strange characters up there, all of which are available for naming your files.

The only problem with using the Extended ASCII set comes when trying to access the files. You must remember which Alt key combo you originally entered, or keep a chart on the wall. Granted, for file security, this is pretty good. For example, a file named with three "blank" characters won't show up on a directory listing. It will take a while for a snoop to figure out what's going on.

Wildcards

When working with files, remember that you have wildcards that will let you refer to a group of files with similar names. In the previous section, *.TBL was used to represent all files with a .TBL extension—no matter what their filename.

The two basic wildcards are: the asterisk (*), which represents a group of characters, and the question mark (?) which represents a single character in the filename.

This material, and using these wildcards, should already be familiar to you. Unfortunately, there really are no DOS secrets about using the wildcards. But there are some DOS stupidities.

The * wildcard is designed to represent from one to eight or three characters, depending on which side of the dot separator you put it on. But note that * just doesn't represent a group of characters—it represents all characters up to the last one. For example:

```
M*BAR.DAT
```

Some users may suppose that all files starting with an M then having the three letters BAR in the filename and DAT as an extension will match the wildcard. Nope! The above actually translates into:

```
M*.DAT
```

The * wildcard is really stupid about this. In fact, internally, DOS translates the * into a corresponding number of question marks. So DOS will convert the original M*BAR.DAT into:

```
M???????.DAT
```

Note here that the question mark doesn't represent an absolute character. The seven question marks above can represent from one to seven characters. A filename doesn't need to use all positions taken by a single ? to match perfectly. (Kinda lame; don't you agree?)

Directory Wildcards

There are two wildcards that are used when working with directories. Without getting too far into the next section, DOS makes use of the dot and dot-dot wildcards to represent the current directory and parent directory, respectively.

You've seen the following two files at the top of every DOS directory listing:

```
.     ⟨DIR⟩     9-24-88     4:26p
..    ⟨DIR⟩     9-24-88     4:26p
```

These two directory ("DIR") listings represent the current directory and its parent, or the directory above the current directory (except the root directory, which has no parent).

You can use . and .. in DOS as abbreviations for the current directory and the parent. For example:

```
DIR .
```

This command causes DOS to list all files in the current directory. But it's not that convincing. Although DIR *.* does the same thing, so does DIR all by itself. Instead, try something more drastic:

```
DEL .
```

This tells DOS to delete the current directory—the same as DEL *.*. To prove it, type the following at the command prompt:

```
DEL .
Are you sure (Y/N)?
```

Type "N" and ENTER. (Unless you really do want to delete all files in the current directory.)

The dot-dot abbreviation can be used to access the parent directory. However, its best use is with the CD command, covered in the next section.

WORKING WITH SUBDIRECTORIES

DOS 2.0 and the PC/XT introduced PC computing to the world of the hard drive. The PC/XT provided the hardware necessary and DOS 2.0 gave us the software to tame the wilderness. But the manuals didn't give us a clue as to what to do with it.

Today you can have a hard drive with thousands of files on it. Each one of them is restricted to the same 8-dot-3 naming conventions. But who knows what's in them? Who knows which applications created them? Where do they go?

That job is up to you. You have to organize your hard drive into work areas called subdirectories. Without them, you'd have one big disk full of files—a mess. DOS provides the tools but no rules for working with subdirectories.

There are three DOS commands used to create and manipulate subdirectories. They're based on similar commands in the UNIX operating system:

Command	Abbrev.	UNIX	Function
MKDIR	MD	mkdir	Make/create a directory
CHDIR	CD	cd	Change directories
CHDIR	CD	pwd	Display current directory
RMDIR	RD	rmdir	Remove/delete a directory

Figure 8: Shown are DOS's subdirectory commands.

Using these commands is no secret. But how you put them to use is a mystery to many DOS users.

MKDIR, or MD, is used to create a directory. The directory is named just like a file, though most people don't put an extension on a directory name.

CHDIR, or CD, is used to move between directories. By itself, it displays the name of the current directory.

RMDIR, or RD, is used to remove a directory. You must first delete all files and any subdirectories before deleting a directory.

Of the three, you'll use CHDIR, or CD, most often. MKDIR is used to set up your subdirectories. But once that's done, CD becomes your autopilot, steering you between the subdirectories.

Pathnames

You can't begin to discuss subdirectories without covering pathnames.

A pathname is like a filename, but it also gives a disk drive and subdirectory location; the path you need to take to find a file or group of files.

The pathname has three elements:

- The disk drive
- The subdirectories
- The filename

The disk drive consists of the drive letter, followed by a colon. The subdirectories consist of all subdirectories on the drive in which a file is located—the "parent" subdirectories. And finally, the name of a file in question.

The filename is really optional. You can use a pathname simply to refer to a subdirectory on disk. But when a program requests a full pathname, or when you're copying files and you need to get very specific, then a full pathname—including the filename—is required.

The subdirectories are the most cryptic part of the pathname. That listing starts first with the root directory, the main directory on the disk drive, which is represented by a single backslash, \.

Following the root are the names of all other subdirectories as they branch from the root. Each subdirectory is separated by a backslash. The final one need not be followed by a backslash—unless it's followed by a filename.

```
C:\WP\BOOKS\SECRET\CHAP04.DOC
```

The above pathname can be separated out (or "parsed") as follows:

The disk drive = C:
The subdirectories = \WP\BOOKS\SECRET\
The filename = CHAP04.DOC

The file CHAP04.DOC is on Drive C. It's immediately located in the SECRET directory, which is a subdirectory of BOOKS, which is a subdirectory of WP, which is a subdirectory of the root directory. If you were to draw a chart of sorts, this is where the file would be located:

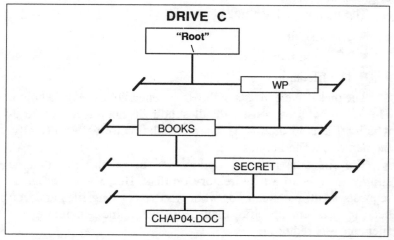

Figure 9: C:\WP\BOOKS\SECRET\CHAP04.DOC.

Other subdirectories and files have been eliminated from the chart, to make presentation clearer.

If you just wanted to specify the location of the subdirectory BOOKS, you could use the following path:

```
C:\WP\BOOKS
```

If you wanted to refer to all files and subdirectories in BOOKS, you could use the following:

```
C:\WP\BOOKS\*.*
```

Note, however, that this only refers to files and subdirectories within BOOKS itself—not the files in subdirectories below it. DOS can only reference one subdirectory at a time.

Making Directories

MKDIR is used to create a new directory. (Most people will use MD.)

Each disk has one main, root directory. Other directories branch off of the root, and other directories can branch off these. In the end, the structure resembles a tree, with the root at the top and subdirectories branching down. (It's an upside-down tree.)

To make a directory, use the same naming conventions as when creating a file. The directory is created by MD as follows:

```
MD pathname\directory
```

Pathname is the name of the directory's parent—the location from which the new subdirectory will branch. Normally, it's not used—you use CD to move to the new directory's parent, and then create the directory without a *pathname*.

Directory is the name of the directory to be created:

```
MD WP
```

This creates the subdirectory WP (probably for word processing) in the current directory. If you wanted to put WP off the root directory, you could specify a path as follows:

```
MD \WP
```

This creates a subdirectory WP in the root directory of the current drive. The root directory is specified via the single back-slash.

Making directories is the best way to organize your hard disk. You can create a subdirectory for each of your applications, create data subdirectories for your applications' data files, or create subdirectories for the files you work on. But before you go nuts with it, you need to consider some type of organization. This is covered in the last part of this chapter.

Changing Directories

CHDIR is the most common of DOS's three directory commands. (Most people will type CD.) CD has two uses:

When used by itself, CD will display your current directory (actually the pathname):

```
CD

C:\
```

In the above example, the CD command displayed C:\, which is the current subdirectory. (Actually it's the current path.)

The second use of CD is directory migration. It will move you instantly to any subdirectory on the hard drive.

For example, suppose you're in the subdirectory PROJECTS under the LOTUS subdirectory. (Refer to Figure 9.)

If you want to change to the subdirectory \WP\BOOKS, you enter the following at the DOS prompt:

```
CD \WP\BOOKS
```

Ta da! You're there.

Most people are rather dumb when it comes to the CD command. They feel they have to "climb the entire tree" rather than type in the full pathname of where they want to go. So instead of a single CD \WP\BOOKS command, they may type:

```
CD \LOTUS
CD \
CD \WP
CD BOOKS
```

That's five commands and quite a few extra keystrokes, when the direct method will get you to the same place and take less time.

A nifty shortcut you can use when navigating through your tree structure is the dot-dot abbreviation for the parent directory. Remember, dot-dot stands for the parent directory. So to move to the parent directory, you could type:

```
CD ..
```

No matter where you are (except for the root), that command will move you "up" one level in the subdirectory structure. Often it's quicker to type than the parent directory's name—which must also be a full pathname.

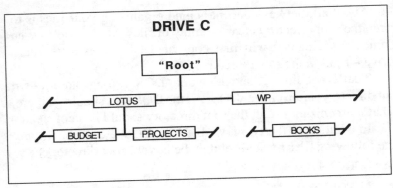

Figure 10: Shown is a partial subdirectory structure.

BUILDING A WORKING STRUCTURE

There is a point and purpose behind having all the subdirectory commands. It's organization. A hard drive is a big place to store a lot of little files. If the hard drive limited itself to only the root directory, you could have a mess of some hundreds of files. This has the following negative effects:

- There would be filename conflicts
- Directory access would be slow
- It's just a bad idea

Computers are supposed to make your life easier. Wading through a 500 file directory listing is stupid. It shows bad organization and it makes DOS run a heck of a lot slower. So instead of putting up with that, you should take advantage of subdirectories and organize your files.

DOS makes no rules about organizing your files. The DOS manual doesn't even provide good working models (which is why so many people don't practice organization). Other operating systems, OS/2 and UNIX, have definite organization strategies. But you're on your own with DOS.

KEEP THE ROOT CLEAN

About all, the key concept behind organizing your files is to keep the root directory clean—empty of files. Most people (even some "consultants") will first copy all DOS's files to the hard drive—right in the root directory!

That's not how it should work. DOS belongs in its own subdirectory, often called \DOS. All the DOS files should go there. That's organization. But the root directory should be kept clean.

In addition to the two invisible files DOS uses to boot, only the following files must absolutely be in your root directory:

```
CONFIG.SYS

AUTOEXEC.BAT
```

COMMAND.COM doesn't need to be in the root. You can specify a new location for it in CONFIG.SYS. But even so, AUTOEXEC.BAT needs to be in the root. CONFIG.SYS is in the root because it's loaded way before DOS sets up any disk interaction. It cannot be moved.

Other than those two (or three) files, you should only have subdirectories listed in your root directory. And then, you should not have more than a dozen subdirectories—at the max. You're just not being organized if you have a lot of subdirectories in the root directory.

A PLAN OF ATTACK

It's hard to describe subdirectory organization without examples. Granted, each user's case is individual. But there are some general organizational strategies you can take. The following shows three strategies that work best for some people. You can pick one for yourself, or use a combination.

Notice how each of these examples puts the DOS files in their own DOS subdirectory. Of all the ways to organize your applications and files, finding a place for DOS is top priority.

Simple Subdirectory Structure

A simple subdirectory structure involves only a few subdirectories off the root directory, one containing each major application you use. Under those subdirectories you put your data subdirectories, containing your worksheets, documents, and other files you create using the applications.

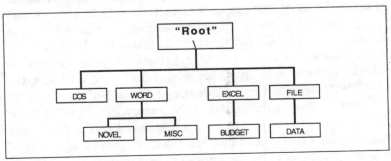

Figure 11: Shown is a simple subdirectory structure.

Figure 11 shows an example of a simple subdirectory structure. Each major application (and DOS) has its own private subdirectory off the root directory. Most applications you install will want to install themselves this way. Below each application's directory are data subdirectories. Note how they're named to reflect their contents. Also, note that there can be more than one subdirectory under each application.

The \WORD\MISC subdirectory is an interesting example. Quite often you'll find you have a variety of files that don't fall under any category. In that case, you can shuffle them off to a \MISC subdirectory somewhere. When enough of them start to relate, you can move (copy and delete the originals) them over to a new subdirectory.

Complex Structure

A complex structure is usually for someone with a lot of files on their drive. Figure 12 should give you an idea of what a complex subdirectory structure should look like.

Figure 12 is only a partial map of the subdirectory structure. Basically, it is for people with a lot of applications. Rather than stick them all off the root directory, special subdirectories are created for each major category of application. For example, all word processors are put in \WP; all programming languages would be put in \PROGRAM; graphics go in \GRAPHICS.

You should also note that all files dealing with the basic system are put in a \SYSTEM subdirectory. This includes DOS, a UTIL subdirectory for utilities, and a MEMRES subdirectory for memory resident software. Other subdirectories could be added to \SYSTEM, each for a specific device or add-on's files.

Finally, there's the \JUNK subdirectory. (Personally, I use \TEMP.) It's always nice to have a designated spot to put things that you don't really need but aren't quite ready to erase. \JUNK is also a great spot to put backups of important files, to hold them while you're doing re-arranging and housekeeping.

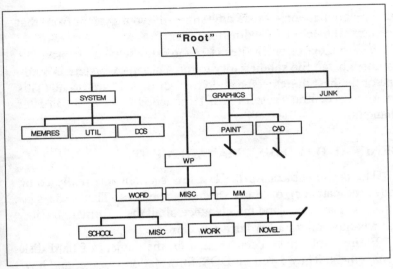

Figure 12: Shown is a complex subdirectory structure.

This type of structure is quite flexible; there's always a place for new files in a subdirectory somewhere. In fact, it keeps the root and all the subdirectories clean. Another possibility would be a communications subdirectory, COMM. Under that could be a \DOWNLOAD and \UPLOAD subdirectory, one for script files, another for macros. There's no limit to how you can get organized. The more organized your system is, the most efficiently it will run.

Batch File Central

The only improvement upon the previous example is by adding a special \BATCH subdirectory, usually in your \SYSTEM subdirectory (or under DOS if you don't have a \SYSTEM). How does this improve?

Because the complex subdirectory structure has a lot of files and subdirectories, moving around and running files can be a pain. So to make things easier, you write a batch file for each of the programs and applications on your hard drive. That way, you can run any application—or do anything—on your system from that one central batch file subdirectory.

The subject of batch files is covered in the next chapter. But having a batch file subdirectory to run a complex system is really one of the best things you can do for a crowded hard drive. (This "batch file central" system will be touched upon again in later chapters.)

GENERAL HARD DISK MANAGEMENT

The entire subject for the last few sections has really come under the category of Hard Disk Management. That's the systematic organization and maintenance of all the information (files and whatnot) on your hard drive system.

Entire books have been written on the subject of hard disk management. They dwell on DOS, information storage, and how to organize a hard disk. But basically the subject matter boils down to the following three things:

- Organization
- Housekeeping
- Backup

Organization

Organization is subdirectories. It's keeping all your files organized into subdirectories, and keeping the subdirectories organized. But that's not all.

A good hard disk should have no more than 12 subdirectories in the root directory. Carrying this further, there should be no more than 12 subdirectories in any one directory. In fact, having more than six subdirectories is a sign of poor organization.

DOS provides an upper limit of 64 characters in a pathname. If you give all your subdirectories the full eight-character filename, that means you can at least go seven levels deep. Use it!

Keep everything organized and you'll discover that you can find information quicker, and that DOS responds a lot quicker.

The same holds true for files. Sometimes it's necessary to have some 50 or so files in a single directory. But any more than that is getting ridiculous. Nothing bogs a system down like too many files in a subdirectory.

Keep organized!

Housekeeping

Housekeeping is the day-to-day maintenance and management of the files on your system. It involves deleting old files, moving files around, installing applications, formatting diskettes, and so on. Disk housekeeping and maintenance are primary parts of keeping your system in top shape.

To assist in housekeeping, many enterprising programmers have written hard disk utilities. A few of the better ones to look into are listed below:

- *The Mace Utilities*
  Fifth Generation Systems
  10049 N. Reiger Road
  Baton Rouge, LA 70809
  (504) 291-7221

- *Magellan*
  Lotus Development Corp.
  55 Cambridge Parkway
  Cambridge, MA 02142
  (617) 577-8500

- *The Norton Commander*
  The Norton Utilities
  Peter Norton Computing
  100 Wilshire Blvd., 9th Floor
  Santa Monica, CA 90401
  (213) 319-2000

- *PC Tools Deluxe*
  Central Point Software, Inc.
  15220 NW Greenbrier Pkwy., #200
  Beaverton, OR 97006
  (503) 690-8090

- *VCache*
  VOpt
  Golden Bow Systems
  2665 Ariane Drive, Suite 207
  San Diego, CA 92117
  (800) 284-3269

- *XTreePro Gold*
  Executive Systems, Inc.
  4330 Santa Fe Road
  San Luis Obispo, CA 93104
  (805) 541-0604

Backup

Finally, there's backup. That's the archiving of information on the hard drive to floppies for safe keeping—or "just in case."

Backup is a chore. No one likes to do it, but it comes in handy sometimes. Hard drives can break down and the backup is the only copy with which to reconstruct data. Those who have neglected to backup and experience a hard disk crash now backup religiously.

Part of the problem with backup is that most people assume you need to backup the full hard drive every day. Instead, you need only to work out a backup schedule. For example, backup only those files you've worked on today—and for the rest of the week. Then, at the end of the week, or as frequently as once a month, backup the entire system.

The object is to always have at least a working copy of the hard drive "just in case" at any time. That way, you can reconstruct the hard disk, and all your precious data, at any given time, losing only maybe today's work.

Backup isn't a secret; it's just good advice.

SUMMARY

File organization is a big part of DOS, especially in light of the hard drive. There are some secrets involved, but most of the "secrets" are simply using the tools DOS already gives you: Name your files properly; implement subdirectories to hold similar files; and organize your subdirectories to make working with a hard drive easier.

The next chapter touches upon batch files, which are DOS programs that you can write yourself. The power of batch files is an underlying theme throughout this book. You'll see how they become more useful and handy in the latter chapters.

CHAPTER 5

Batch Files

Batch files can certainly come in handy. They have many uses, from installing new applications to performing routine chores to running programs on your system. But the best part is, anyone can create a batch file—a type of DOS program—to use on their system.

This chapter is about batch files. The information here just barely scratches the surface of what batch files can do. Why? Because it's a programming language and has depth and complexity that would be too much to detail here. But for a good introduction—plus some secrets—batch files are covered here in three sections:

- What are batch files?
- How to make a batch file
- Examples

The first section offers a general discussion of batch files, plus all the individual parts of this mini-programming language (but don't let "programming language" scare you off!). Next comes the subject of creating batch files, and finally, some interesting examples you can put to use right away.

WHAT ARE BATCH FILES?

Batch files are text files. But the text they contain is in the form of DOS commands, application names, special batch file programming directives, and just about anything else you'd type on the command line.

Batch files get their name from older computers that used "batch processing." The computer would be given a series of instructions, usually on a stack of programming cards—a batch of cards. The computer would chew the cards up (sometimes literally) and process them, eventually spitting out an answer (more likely an error code).

IBM needed some type of batch processing ability in DOS to perform repetitive diagnostic tests with their first PC. Microsoft, who produced DOS for IBM, decided to take the tests further and make them into a batch language. So in addition to processing a series of diagnostic tests, the batch files could store and process any DOS command.

Today, batch files are text files that store DOS commands—anything you'd type on the command line. For example, suppose you have a stack of 15 diskettes and for each one you need to type the following DOS commands:

```
COPY A:\*.EXE C:\PROGRAMS
COPY A:\*.COM C:\PROGRAMS
COPY A:\*.TXT C:\TEXT
```

(This is a rather bizarre example.)

Rather than type those commands each time, you can put each one of them—in text form—into a batch file. Then instead of typing all those commands, you simply type the batch file's name and the computer does all the work for you (like it's supposed to).

The only thing making a batch file different from other text files on disk is its filename extension. All batch files have the BAT filename extension.

BATCH FILE CONTENTS

Creating a batch file is covered in the next section. They're really nothing more than text files containing DOS commands. But that .BAT filename extension does play a major role in how DOS treats them.

Other than the file format basics, the following items can be placed into a batch file:

- DOS commands
- Application names
- Batch file directives
- Variables

DOS commands are anything you'd type on the command line. After all, a batch file is only a little more than a collection of DOS commands, all wrapped neatly into a text file.

Application names also find their way into batch files. Since you can type an application name on the DOS command line, this only makes sense.

The most important, and useful, item to go into a batch file are special batch file directives. These are part of the batch file programming language DOS uses that makes batch files more than just a collection of DOS commands. Using these batch file directives, you can turn batch files into an almost-programming language, complete with repetitive loops and decision making abilities. (But no math; batch files have no math abilities.)

Finally batch files can take advantage of batch file variables. These come in two flavors: items typed on the command line after the batch file, and environment variables.

It's possible to get quite complex with batch files. The subject is really simple, but like most simple things it can build and build until it gets rather complex. This chapter can only give you so many hints as to what batch files can do. If you'd like more advanced information, I'd recommend a book I wrote on batch file

programming: *Advanced MS-DOS Batch File Programming* from
TAB Books (ISBN 0-8306-3197-6).

Don't let the title scare you: It's not complex stuff, just
intended for a more experienced DOS user. It will give you all the
information necessary to create truly useful batch files. Otherwise,
the following two sections will elaborate on batch file commands
and variables.

Batch File Commands

In addition to DOS commands and application names, the
following are batch file commands specific to the batch file
programming language.

There are eight words in the batch file programming language.
Each of them, along with a description and example is provided in
the Figure 13.

Of these commands, the most popular will be ECHO, FOR,
GOTO, IF, PAUSE and REM.

Command	Description	Example
CALL	Runs a second batch file	CALL *filename*.BAT
ECHO	Displays text/ Turns ECHO on or off	ECHO *text*... ECHO ON / ECHO OFF
FOR	Repeats DOS commands for a group of files	FOR %*v* in (*filename*...) DO *command*
GOTO	Branches execution to a label	GOTO *label*
IF	Executes a command based on a certain condition	IF *condition command*
PAUSE	Displays a pause message, waits for a key to be struck	PAUSE
REM	Allows comments to be inserted into the batch file	RAM *comment*...
SHIFT	Shifts command line variables	SHIFT

Figure 13: Shown above are batch file commands.

ECHO

ECHO is used traditionally to start a batch file. The command ECHO OFF turns off display of the batch file, which is normally echoed to the screen as each line is executed. With ECHO OFF, the batch file runs silent.

ECHO ON can also be used, though it's rarely done. Instead, the only other purpose for ECHO is to display text on the screen. ECHO displays all text following it—unless you use ECHO alone. Normally, you'd suspect this would echo a blank line. Nope. It merely states the current status of the ECHO command, "ECHO is off" or "ECHO is on."

Starting with DOS 3.3, the @ (at) batch file command can be used in place of ECHO OFF—but for one line only. All lines in a batch file you precede with the @ sign won't be echoed to the display, no matter what the status of ECHO.

FOR

The FOR command repeats a single DOS command for a group of files you specify. Used with FOR is a batch file variable, preceded by percentage signs, that is the placeholder for the group of files. For example:

```
FOR %%A in (*.TXT) DO TYPE %%A
```

In this example, the group of files is designated between the parenthesis, *.TXT. The DOS command follows "DO." And the variable representing the group of files is %%A. The result of this command will have DOS locate all files matching *.TXT in the current directory, and for each of them it will issue the TYPE command, listing the file to the screen.

Another example:

```
FOR %%G IN (*.COM *.EXE *.BAT) DO DIR %%G
```

This command will list all COM, EXE and BAT files in the current directory.

GOTO

The GOTO command branches batch file execution to a specific *label*. The label follows GOTO, and it also exists elsewhere in the batch file on a line by itself, preceded by a colon (:). For example:

```
GOTO THERE
ECHO THIS LINE WON'T BE DISPLAYED
:THERE
```

In the above example, the second line (ECHO) won't be executed. Instead, DOS will process the batch file, branching to ":THERE" as dictated by the GOTO command.

IF

The IF command is used to make a decision. The decision is based on either a comparison, ERRORLEVEL variable, or an EXIST test. For example:

```
IF %COMSPEC%==C:\COMMAND.COM ECHO Okay
```

In this example, IF tests to see if the environment variable COMSPEC is equal to C:\COMMAND.COM. If so, the ECHO command is executed. Note that two equal signs are used in this type of comparison.

```
IF ERRORLEVEL 5 GOTO BOOBOO
```

In this example, the ERRORLEVEL variable is tested. Some programs return an ERRORLEVEL variable when they're canceled due to some error or problem. Your batch files can examine the error by using IF to compare the ERRORLEVEL variable. In the above example, if the ERRORLEVEL of the previous program is 5 *or greater*, then batch file execution branches to the BOOBOO label. Note that the comparison is for a value equal to or greater than that listed.

```
IF EXIST *.BAT ECHO There are batch files here!
```

The EXIST test determines if any matching filenames are found. In the above example, EXIST checks to see if any filenames matching *.BAT are in the current directory. If so, the ECHO command is executed. If not, batch file execution continues with the next line.

PAUSE

The PAUSE command is used to pause the display, requesting that the user press any key to continue. PAUSE often finds its place after ECHO'd warning messages or after a long screen full of text. For example, if the batch file was about to delete something, you could write a few lines such as:

```
ECHO You're about to delete all the files!
ECHO Press Control-Break to stop, or
PAUSE
DEL *.*
```

The visual effect this produces on the screen is:

```
You're about to delete all the files!
Press Control-Break to stop, or
Strike a key when ready . . .
```

PAUSE produces the "Strike a key when ready . . ." prompt, and then waits. If you press Control-Break, the batch file will ask: "Terminate batch job (Y/N)?" to which you can press "N" to return to DOS and stop the batch file.

REM

The REM command does nothing. When the batch file is executed, the batch interpreter skips over it. However, REM is good for including comments and REMarks in your batch file:

```
REM This batch file will clean up my hard drive
REM Written on January 15, 1993
```

(etc.)

The REMarks are for you, later when you want to rework the batch file, or examine it to see what it's doing. They aren't necessary, but REMarks have traditionally been a part of every computer programming language, primarily to give computer programming teachers something to mark you down for when you forget to include them.

Other commands are explained in the DOS manual (though I hate to refer you there). But instead, why not check out my batch file programming book? (Hint, hint.)

Variables

Batch files also make use of variables, which are temporary storage places for strings of text. Note that batch files only use text variables. Since they don't do math, numbers aren't stored in batch files. (Numbers as text can be in variables, but not numbers as values.)

There are two types of batch file variables:

- Environment variables
- Command line parameters

Environment variables are discussed in the following chapter. When you use them with batch files, remember to enclose them in percent signs. For example:

```
%HOME%
```

Also, they're primarily used with IF, though if you use ECHO with an environment variable, it will echo the variable's contents to the display. (The same applies to command line parameters and ECHO.)

Command line parameters are variables that represent anything typed on the command line with the batch file name. They're numbered %0 though %9, with each %-number representing a single word on the command line. For example:

```
WP LETTER1.DOC
```

In this example, two items are typed on the command line, WP (really WP.BAT) and LETTER1.DOC. The command line variables representing those two items are %0 and %1. %0 represents WP, and %1 represents LETTER1.DOC.

These command line variables come in handy when referencing items typed on the command line after a batch file. You'll see ample examples in the last section of this chapter.

HOW TO MAKE A BATCH FILE

Batch files are text files. To create them you have three choices:

- A text editor
- A word processor
- COPY CON

The best choice for creating and working on batch files is a text editor. A text editor is like a word processor, but it only deals with plain text files—like batch files and other text (or "source code") files required by all programming languages.

Text editors lack text formatting features, such as centering, bold, underline, and margins. They also lack fancy printing, fonts, headers and footers, notes, and graphics that proliferate in all word processing packages today. They're ideally suited for editing and creating batch files—and they're cheap!

The most common editor is the horrid DOS EDLIN program. But other, cheaper editors exist that do a much better job. One of the best (and least expensive) is *QEdit*. It's available from Sem-Ware, 4343 Shallowford Rd., Suite C-3, Marietta, GA, 30062-5003; (404) 641-9002, $40.

Word processors can be used to create batch files. But that's like using a dump truck in a supermarket instead of a shopping cart. Word processing software is overburdened with features that make editing batch files awkward. But it can be done.

If you want to use a word processor to create and edit batch files, remember to save the batch file in the plain text, DOS text, or ASCII text mode. Also, type ENTER at the end of each line.

Finally, there's the old COPY CON "function." Quick and dirty batch files are made a dozen to the day using COPY CON *filename*.BAT. For two or three line batch files, nothing could be easier. (Just remember the Control-Z to end the file.)

BATCH FILE EXAMPLES

There is no end to the variety and versatility that batch files provide. Books and computer magazine columns are devoted to the subject. But rather than fill space here, I thought to give you four examples of the variety and usefulness batch files provide.

DS.BAT—Directory Sort

This batch file displays a sorted directory listing, plus a pause between each screen page.

```
1: ECHO OFF
2: REM Sort directory
3: DIR | SORT > $$TEMP
4: MORE < $$TEMP
5: DEL $$TEMP
```

Line 1 turns ECHO OFF. If you have DOS 3.3, you might want to put an @ sign in front of ECHO OFF, as in: @ECHO OFF. This suppresses the display and keeps the screen neat.

Line 2 is a comment, telling you what the batch file will do.

Line 3 through 5 perform the sort. First, output from a sorted directory is redirected to a temporary file on disk called $$TEMP. That file is then displayed using the MORE filter in line 4. Finally, the temporary file is deleted in line 5.

WP.BAT—Running an Application

This batch file is used to run an application, for example from a batch file subdirectory in a complex subdirectory organization scheme (see Chapter Four). The program run is WP.EXE a word processor. Note how command line variables are used to represent any documents typed after the batch file.

```
01: ECHO OFF
02: WP\WP %1
```

It's really quite simple how this works. The first line turns off the echo. The second line runs the word processing file—plus the filename specified. Any program can be run this way. And if you need to perform more setup, those commands can be included in the batch file as well.

MOVE.BAT—Move Files

One command DOS doesn't include is the MOVE command. It's just a combination COPY and ERASE command, first copying the file(s) to a new location and then deleting the original(s). A batch file can do that:

```
01: ECHO OFF
02: REM MOVE FILES FROM %1 TO %2
03: IF %1NOTHING==NOTHING GOTO WARNING
04: IF %2NOTHING==NOTHING GOTO WARNING
05: ECHO Moving Files...
06: COPY %1 %2 > NUL
07: DEL %1 < C:\SYSTEM\BATCH\YES > NUL
08: ECHO Files moved
09: GOTO END
10: :WARNING
11: ECHO Please specify a source and
    destination filename
12: :END
```

This batch file is fairly complex. It uses a lot of batch file tricks, including command line variables, I/O redirection, and a second file on disk called "YES."

Line 1 turns the ECHO off. Line 2 is a comment explaining that files will be moved from the first command line option to the second. So the format of the MOVE "command" is:

```
MOVE source destination
```

Or, as an example:

```
MOVE C:\WP\KILL C:\JUNK
```

Lines 3 and 4 use the IF command to test if nothing has been entered. If so, the GOTO command causes the batch file to jump up to line 10, the :WARNING label, and display a message. If not, then both of MOVE's parameters have been specified, and the program continues.

Line 5 displays the message "Moving Files...", which lets you know what's going on.

Line 6 performs the initial COPY command, copying the files from the source to the destination. The output from this command is redirected to the NUL device, which means any "xx File(s) copied" messages won't be displayed on the screen.

Line 7 deletes the original files. But note how I/O redirection is used. When you DELete files, DOS may sometimes ask "Are you sure?" to which you must press "Y" or "N." The keystrokes "Y+ENTER" have been stored in a file YES in the \SYS-TEM\BATCH subdirectory. Input redirection supplies them for the DEL command. And the output (if any) is again redirected to the NUL device.

Line 8 echoes the message "Files moved," letting you know the operation is complete. Then the GOTO in line 9 skips over the warning/error message display and ends the batch file in line 12.

Whew! What a batch file! But it just goes to show you the complexity and detail that the batch file basics can provide. It's no secret, but you can do amazing things with them. Such as the following:

KILL.BAT—Delete Files (The Safe Way)

Both ERASE and DEL are used to remove files. But unless you have a file un-delete utility, the file is gone forever. A safer way is to implement the KILL.BAT file, and use KILL to delete your files.

The KILL batch file copies files to a \TRASH subdirectory, then deletes the originals. The end result is the same; the file is gone from your disk. But instead of being totally gone, it's in the \TRASH subdirectory. From there, you can delete it at a later date.

```
01: ECHO OFF
02: :START
03: IF %1NOTHING==NOTHING GOTO END
04: COPY %1 C:\TRASH>NUL
05: DEL %1 < C:\SYSTEM\BATCH\YES > NUL
06: ECHO %1 Killed
07: SHIFT
08: GOTO START
09: :END
```

This batch file uses a programming trick known as a "loop" to execute over and over. Both GOTO and IF provide the mechanism for the loop, but in the end you get an interesting command. For example, to use KILL you can type the following on the command line:

```
C:\WP\MISC> KILL JUNK *.LTR MISC JANE*.*
```

This directs KILL to remove the file JUNK, all files *.LTR, the file MISC, and all files matching JANE*.*. After pressing ENTER, you will see:

```
JUNK Killed
*.LTR Killed
MISC Killed
JANE*.* Killed
```

What's new in this batch file that wasn't found in the MOVE.BAT file is the SHIFT command in line 7. It shifts the command line variables "over one," subtracting one from their value. So the original %2 (*.LTR above) becomes %1. From there, it can be acted on in the program.

Line 3 does the testing to see if any files exist to be deleted. If so, they're copied to \TRASH and the original is deleted. If not, execution branches to the :END label and the batch file is done.

Pretty nifty, eh?

SUMMARY

This chapter just begins to skim the surface of what batch files can do. They really are the glue that binds all DOS secrets together. From the basis for running an organized hard disk, to creating interesting utilities such as MOVE and KILL, a lot can be done with batch files.

Batch files will come in handy throughout the remainder of this book. The following chapter is on memory and then environment. The variables you can create in the environment have a direct role to play with batch files.

PART THREE

CHAPTER 6

Memory and the Environment

This chapter covers two different subjects. The first is memory, which becomes more and more important because DOS is severely restricted in the way it can use it. The second is the environment, which is related to memory in a general sense, but actually it's a storage location for DOS in memory.

This chapter discusses memory and the environment in two sections, appropriately enough:

- Memory
- The environment

Memory isn't really something with which you can pull any DOS tricks. It's just something you should know about. The environment, on the other hand, is full of surprises. It's related to memory in that it uses memory. But otherwise, this is just a two-in-one chapter. Like a Tootsie Roll Pop.

MEMORY

Memory is important in a PC because DOS really doesn't give you that much of it. True, in 1981, 640K was gobs of memory—ten times what the old CP/M computers had. But today, with a '386 microprocessor able to grab up to four gigabytes (billions of bytes) worth of memory, 640K isn't enough. Especially for high-end applications—CAD, desktop publishing, and so on—memory is tight.

There are memory solutions out there. But that's the subject of another book. For your DOS guruhood diploma, you'll need to know the following things about your PC's memory:

- How DOS uses memory
- Memory resident programs
- Shelling
- Extended and expanded memory

There are many secrets here, but few tricks. Yet all this is still important information you should know about.

How DOS Uses Memory

DOS was written for the original IBM PC, introduced in 1981. The original PC used an 8088 microprocessor that could only access one megabyte, or 1,024K, of RAM. Because of that, and because all PCs since have maintained compatibility with that system, all DOS computers today adhere to the same limitations. Even the PC/AT, with its 80286 that can use up to 16 megabytes of RAM, or a 386 PC that can use up to four gigabytes of RAM, are all still limited to the one megabyte arrangement under DOS. Needless to say, this causes some frustrations.

Within that one megabyte, certain areas of memory are devoted to certain things. The largest hunk, 640K, is devoted to DOS for running programs and storing data. This is known as *Conventional DOS memory*. The rest of the basic one megabyte, 384K, is referred to as *High DOS memory*. It contains memory for the video display, the hard disk controller, and your PC's BIOS. There's some breathing room up there as well, for system expansion, network cards, and so on.

The way most computer gurus look at memory is via the fabled computer memory map. A memory map for the PC is shown in Figure 14.

The problem with this map is the line located at 640K. Even though you may have a '386 computer, capable of accessing megabytes of RAM directly, you're still limited to only 640K under DOS. This has caused a lot of users some severe frustration anxiety. Being limited by DOS is a problem, especially in the light of what these new, faster microprocessors can do.

There are solutions to the memory situation, a few of which are covered near the end of this section. But put that aside for a moment and mull over the following background information.

Memory Resident Programs

When you type the name of a program at the DOS prompt, DOS loads it into memory. Right from the start, the program occupies space in your system's basic 640K of RAM. Additional space is used for the program's data, for your spreadsheet (which is a major memory hog), the document you're working on in your word processor, or any

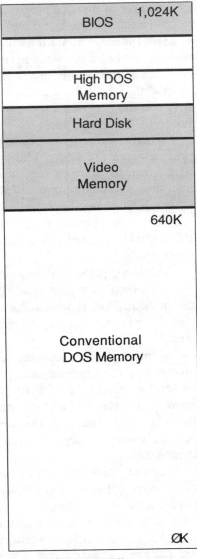

Figure 14: Shown is DOS's memory map.

of a number of things a program can use memory for.

When the program is done, it tells DOS it wants to quit. DOS releases the memory used by the program, making it available to the next program you want to run.

This is the way memory is used in the PC: Each program "owns" the whole lot of RAM when it runs, dividing the space up between the program itself and the data you generate with the program. But things don't have to be that way.

When some programs quit, they may stay in memory. These programs are the fabled Memory Resident programs you may have. Instead of releasing their memory when they quit, the memory resident program will stay in memory, using up a chunk of it. DOS comes back up "on top" of the memory resident program. And from there, you can run more applications. But the RAM used by the memory resident program is subtracted from the 640K total.

Incidentally, the DOS function call used to quit a program and make it memory resident is called Terminate and Stay Resident in the manual. This is why some marketing people and computer weenies will call memory resident software TSRs. (Ugh, what a term.)

Memory resident software can be useful. In fact, most of it is, always staying in memory and providing you with some function or service lacking in DOS or your other applications. Memory resident software can add new commands to DOS; it can modify the way the computer works, display the time on the screen, or operate a special "pop-up" utility when you press a certain key combination.

The drawbacks to memory resident software are that they take up memory. (That's number one.) But next to using memory, DOS makes no rules governing how memory resident software behaves. DOS was written under the assumption that only one application would be running in the computer at a time. Further, the application itself always assumes that it's in charge. So memory resident programs cause conflicts and occasionally lock up a computer.

Whether you use memory resident software or not is up to you. Currently, the fad seems to be waning. However, some memory resident utilities, such as spell checkers, calculators, notepads, and what not, are still popular.

Shelling

Related to the concept of memory resident software is shelling. Like making a program memory resident, some applications have the ability to quit and leave themselves intact and in memory. They "shell out" to DOS or another application. You can then return to the original application at some later point using a simple DOS command.

Shelling is something few DOS users know about, let alone take advantage of. It's rather hard to understand, but the concept isn't difficult to grasp. Basically, you're quitting the application—but leaving it in memory. It doesn't continue to run, but you're back out at DOS or in some other application.

You can use the second application, manipulate files in DOS, or whatever. Then, when you're done, you use a special command and—ta da!—you're back in the first program, which has safely been suspended in memory all the time.

Many applications feature a shelling feature. It's often called "Shell" or "Exit" or "Exit to DOS" or "Exec" or "Run." If one of your applications has such a command, try it. You'll either find yourself at the DOS prompt—or the application may ask for a program to run. In either case, after you finish the command you'll be in a shell.

To return to the original program, you need to do one of two things. If you've shelled to DOS, you type the EXIT command. If you've shelled to another application, then just quit that application. Either way will return you to the original application from which you shelled.

Note that if you've shelled to DOS, you can work in DOS as you normally would. The only limitation is that your original program is still in memory, so you won't have much RAM left.

You can demonstrate shelling at the command prompt by typing in the name of DOS's command processor: COMMAND.COM. (Make sure it's on the PATH—see the latter part of this chapter.) For example, you can type:

```
C:\ COMMAND.COM
```

You may see something like the following displayed:

```
The IBM Personal Computer DOS
Version 3.30(C)Copyright International
Business Machines Corp 1981, 1987
 (C)Copyright Microsoft Corp 1981, 1987
```

You are now in a "shell." The original COMMAND.COM is still in memory and you're using a second copy.

When you shell to another copy of DOS (COMMAND.COM), a copy of your system's *environment* is made for the new shell. The environment is covered in the last half of this chapter. But for now, you can make a change to the environment to verify that you have indeed shelled. Type the following:

```
PROMPT I am in a shell$g
```

The PROMPT command (covered later) will change your system prompt to:

```
I am in a shell>
```

It's still the same DOS prompt, just different looking. What you've done is to change your DOS environment. But the original environment is still intact in the original copy of COMMAND.COM. To prove it, exit the shell. Type:

```
I am in a shell>EXIT
```

After pressing ENTER, your old DOS prompt—the original COMMAND.COM—will be returned.

Expanded and Extended Memory

There are two ways to get at memory beyond DOS's paltry little 640K. They are Expanded and Extended memory.

Extended memory is memory above one megabyte (the original amount in the first PC). It's only available on 80286 and 80386 systems. Why? Because those processors can directly access that memory. It's all one straight line as far as they're concerned. So any memory you add to your AT, '286 or '386 system above one megabyte is extended memory.

This all sounds like fun, but there's a problem: DOS can't use extended memory. Extended memory is only accessible by the '286 and '386 systems when they operate in their native mode, also known as the *protected mode*. DOS is a *real mode* operating system. It can't use extended memory.

So what is extended memory good for? Nothing! Nothing, under DOS that is. For other operating systems, such as Xenix, UNIX, or OS/2, extended memory comes in very handy. But DOS ignores it. (Still, there's hope. Keep reading.)

Expanded memory is memory beyond one megabyte on a PC/XT-level system. Of course, the PC/XT system can only access one megabyte. But expanded memory cheats a bit. It uses a segment of High DOS memory as a swap area. It can move in chunks of expanded memory into conventional DOS memory, swapping them in and out quite quickly. That way, you can access more than a megabyte of memory on a PC.

The scheme for using expanded memory is known as EMS, the Expanded Memory Specification. It's run by a device driver loaded into CONFIG.SYS (covered in the next chapter). The device driver is known by the name LIM, for Lotus-Intel-Microsoft, the three behemoth companies that developed the EMS standard.

A lot of DOS software takes advantage of EMS memory to do some incredible things. Spreadsheet programs, the original memory hog, can use EMS memory to create amazingly huge worksheets. Desktop publishing and graphics applications use the extra memory to hold their images.

So having EMS memory can really help you get the most out of your system. But this leaves the questions of '286 and '386 computers, which are better by far and already have extended memory, up in the air. What about them?

The answer is that extended memory can be converted to expanded memory. From there, the '286 and '386 systems can access the wealth of EMS software available under DOS—and more. With EMS memory, '386 PCs can do amazing things, including the ability to run several DOS applications at once. But to do this, you need special software and device drivers to convert the extended to expanded memory.

The following list shows some applications and utilities that convert extended into expanded memory.

For changing extended into expanded memory on a PC/AT or '286 machine, check out:

■ *Above DISC*
   Above Software
   3 Hutton Centre, #950
   Santa Ana, CA 92707
   (714) 545-1181

■ *MOVE'EM*
   Qualitas
   7101 Wisconsin Ave, Suite 1386
   Bethesda, MD 20814
   (301) 907-6700

■ *Turbo EMS*
   Merrill-Bryan Enterprises, Inc.
   9770 Carroll Center Road, Suite C
   San Diego, CA 92126
   (619) 689-8611

■ *QRAM*
   Quarterdeck Office Systems
   150 Pico Boulevard
   Santa Monica, CA 90405
   (213) 392-9851

For converting extended to expanded memory (and more!) on a '386 system, try the following:

- *386MAX*
  Qualitas
  7101 Wisconsin Ave, Suite 1386
  Bethesda, MD 20814
  (301) 907-6700

- *QEMM*
  Quarterdeck Office Systems
  150 Pico Boulevard
  Santa Monica, CA 90405
  (213) 392-9851

These addresses and phone numbers are subject to change. It's best to first look for the product at your favorite Software-O-Rama store before calling or contact your local dealers for more information.

THE ENVIRONMENT

The Environment is where DOS keeps important information, like a scratch pad. Because this information can change, either by DOS, applications programs, or you, the environment is stored in memory.

DOS puts information in the environment in the form of an environment variable and a string. Both of these are text, so you can read them via a special DOS command. The same command also creates environment variables. (It's the SET command, covered in the next section.)

The environment variable is used to represent the string either in DOS or in some applications program. For example:

```
MONITOR=color
```

This could be a line in the environment. A program that looks for the MONITOR variable can examine its contents to see that MONITOR is equal to "color". If this is used to determine which type of display you have, and you have monochrome, you might set the variable as:

```
MONITOR=mono
```

Either way, the program will look for the MONITOR variable in the environment and see what you've set it to. Before moving on, note a few things:

The variable name is always in ALL CAPS. DOS makes it that way. So you can create the variable in lower or upper case and DOS will convert it to upper case.

There is no space before or after the equal sign (=). If there is, then it becomes part of the environment variable and string. So be careful!

When referring to an environment variable in a batch file, surround it with percent signs. For example:

```
ECHO %MONITOR%
```

This command will display either "mono" or "color" depending on how the variable is set.

The SET Command

The SET command is your link to the environment. It both lets you place variables into the environment as well as view the contents of the environment. For example, to view your environment, at the DOS prompt type:

```
SET
```

You'll see a list of a few items in your environment (which will vary from PC to PC).

You also place variables into the environment using the SET command. Normally, DOS automatically puts two variables into the environment:

- COMSPEC
- PATH

COMSPEC is the location of COMMAND.COM. But not
exactly. DOS is really dumb about this variable. It will assign
COMSPEC to \COMMAND.COM for the root directory of your
boot disk. Even if you've moved COMMAND.COM to a subdirectory (using a command in CONFIG.SYS, covered in the next
chapter), COMSPEC will still believe it to be in the root. Wrong!

PATH is DOS's search path. It's a list of subdirectories in
addition to the current directory in which DOS will look for
applications and program names you type at the command prompt.
The specifics of PATH are covered later in this chapter.

To use SET to create your own environment variable, you
simply specify SET, followed by the variable name, equal sign,
and what the variable is to be set to. For example:

```
SET MONITOR=mono
```

By itself this seems rather dumb. And it does use memory (one
byte for each character). But some programs require environment
variables to be set. They tell the program where directories are
located, how to name files, and general system configuration. So
if the manual says, "Set the environment variable STATUS to…",
now you know what to do.

To see if the SET command creates a variable, you use the
command SET by itself to display all environment variables. If
you typed in the above command, you may see the following
displayed after typing:

```
COMSPEC=C:\COMMAND.COM
PATH=
MONITOR=mono
```

To remove a variable you simply use SET and the variable
name, but don't assign anything to it. For example:

```
SET MONITOR=
```

This removes the variable and from the environment, freeing
up that much space.

Why do this? Because sometimes you'll see the error message "Out of environment space." DOS makes room for only so many characters in the environment. If you need a bigger environment, there is a command in CONFIG.SYS you can use. Otherwise you should be conservative.

Aside from DOS, batch files, and a few programs, you won't be spending too much time creating environment variables. But two variables are important to you. They are PATH and PROMPT. In fact, PATH and PROMPT are commands by themselves that set environment variables.

The PATH Command

The PATH command is used to both assign and display DOS's current search path. The search path is a list of subdirectories through which DOS will search to look for programs.

PATH is both an environment variable and a command. You can use it both ways. PATH itself assigns a string of subdirectories to DOS's search path. That creates (or replaces) a variable named PATH in the environment. But you can also use SET PATH= to do the same thing. This confuses some people, but there really is no difference between the two commands.

When DOS first starts, it assigns the PATH variable in the environment to nothing. (It doesn't even make a wild guess!) DOS uses the PATH variable each time you type something on the command line. Why? Because that's how DOS looks for programs you want to run.

When you type a command at the command prompt, DOS looks three places:

First, DOS checks to see if the command is an internal DOS command, like CLS or COPY or SET. If so, the command is executed.

Second, DOS checks the current directory for any program files matching the name you entered. It first checks all COM files, then EXE files, then BAT files for a match. If one is found, then that program file is run.

Third, DOS checks all directories listed by the PATH variable. In each one it searches for a COM, then EXE, then BAT file matching the name you typed in at the command prompt.

Only after all three locations have been searched will DOS give you a "Bad command or filename" error message.

PATH comes in handy by letting you specify subdirectories containing commonly used programs. Or, if you're running everything from a batch file subdirectory, you can put its name on the path. That way, from any subdirectory on any drive, you can run any file in your system.

To set a PATH you use the PATH command as follows:

```
PATH subdirectory;subdirectory;...
```

Subdirectory is the name of a subdirectory, such as C:\SYS-TEM\BATCH. Each subdirectory listed on the path is separated by a semicolon. So a path could be something like:

```
PATH C:\DOS;C:\UTIL;C:\123
```

That path has three subdirectories on it: C:\DOS, C:\UTIL, and C:\123. Notice how the full pathname, including drive letter, is specified. Otherwise, if you were on Drive A, DOS would look there for a \DOS subdirectory.

Remember, you can set the PATH using the SET command as well. The following line would do the same thing as the above PATH command:

```
SET PATH=C:\DOS;C:\UTIL;C:\123
```

Note that an equal sign must be specified with SET.

PATH also has a by-itself mode. When typed on the command line by itself, PATH will list your current path:

```
PATH
C:\DOS;C:\UTIL;C:\123
```

The SET command also displays the PATH variable, but that's in addition to every other variable in the environment, which tends to be confusing.

To remove the PATH (if you want to), you can use SET as follows:

```
SET PATH=
```

Or you can simply specify a single semicolon as the PATH:

```
PATH ;
```

Both of these commands reset the PATH down to nothing.

PATH can really be a boon to your system. By setting things up properly, you can access DOS commands, your favorite word processor, or batch files from anywhere on your system. But before moving on, a warning:

Don't get carried away with the PATH!

Most people, the un-organized types, will get all excited and put seven or more subdirectories on their path. "Oh, boy! Now I can even access my *games* from anywhere," they'll shriek with excitement. Wrong!

At the most, put only *three* items on the path. Why? Because DOS will search for COM, EXE and BAT files in each subdirectory you put on the path. I know. I've met computers that "take hours to load software." It turns out the bozo has fourteen subdirectories on the path. Even typing a nonsense word at the command prompt takes DOS weeks before coming back with a "Bad command or filename" error. Just keep it short and sweet on the path.

The PROMPT Command

Throughout this book, the DOS prompt, "C:\" has been used. But that may not be the way the prompt looks on your system. In fact, without otherwise being told, the prompt usually looks like:

```
C>
```

That's just a typical drive letter and the greater-than sign.

The System PROMPT

The system prompt provides a place for input from the user. It's the first thing you become familiar with when you use DOS. Yet, it doesn't necessarily need to be so intimidating.

Normally the system prompt is set to the current drive letter, followed by a greater-than sign:

```
C>
```

But life isn't that boring. Using the PROMPT command you can change the system prompt to just about anything—even including a color prompt straight from the psychedelic '60s.

PROMPT, like PATH, is a dual-mode command that can also be replaced by SET. What PROMPT does is to create a PROMPT variable in the environment, and then assign that variable to a string of PROMPT commands. It's those commands that control how your display works.

The format of the PROMPT command is:

```
PROMPT commands
```

You can stick an equal sign in there if you want to (and if you use SET to set the PROMPT variable, you have to).

If no *commands* are specified, the prompt resets to the current drive letter plus the greater-than sign. Otherwise, there are 13 prompt commands you can use to create a new prompt (see Figure 15 on the following page).

Note that each command is prefixed by a dollar sign. Also, the letters can be in either upper or lower case.

Anything else you stick in with the commands will be displayed as your command prompt verbatim. For example:

```
PROMPT Yes, Sahib?
```

This produces the DOS prompt "Yes, Sahib?" Cute, but not practical.

The most common PROMPT command (aside from the default) is the following:

```
PROMPT $P$G
```

This sets the prompt to the current pathname plus the greater-than sign. It's the way most of the DOS prompts in this book are referenced. With PG, you can always tell which drive and subdirectory you're in by just looking at the command prompt.

Another popular prompt is the following:

```
PROMPT $D$_$T$_$P$G
```

This command displays something like the following:

```
Sun 3-18-1990
16:45:52.24
C:\SYSTEM\BATCH>
```

Command	Displays
$$	$, a dollar sign
$b	l, the pipe character
$d	The current date
$e	The ESC (escape) character prefis
$g	>, the greater-than
$h	Backspace
$1	<, the less-than
$n	The current drive letter
$p	The current pathname
$q	=, the equal sign
$t	The current time
$v	The DOS version number
$_	A carriage return (new line)

Figure 15: Shown above is a table of PROMPT commands.

That's the date ($D) followed by a carriage return ($_) and the time ($T) followed by another carriage return ($_) and finally the current drive and path.

Some people may add the $H command to backspace over the seconds and hundredths of seconds in the time prompt. Prompts like that could look like this:

```
16:45)
```

The command to produce that is:

```
PROMPT $T$H$H$H$H$H$H$G
```

That's six backspaces ($H) in there to cover up the ungainly seconds and hundredths.

The most versatile of these commands is $e, the ESC character. That gives you access to the ANSI screen and cursor controls—provided you have the ANSI.SYS driver in your CONFIG.SYS file.

ANSI.SYS is covered in detail in Chapter Eight. CONFIG.SYS is covered in the next chapter.

SUMMARY

Memory and the environment are two separate things, but they do share a lot of similarities.

With memory, the problem is getting enough of it. There are memory tricks to squeeze more programs into memory. But this chapter only concentrated on memory resident programs and shelling. In addition, the subject of extended and expanded memory was briefly touched upon.

The environment is a more interesting area, especially to a DOS user hungry for secrets. You can use variables in the environment in batch files—or in some of your programs. You'd be surprised how many may take advantage of environment variables.

Aside from the variables, the environment also holds your PATH and PROMPT. These are two areas of DOS that can really make or break a system. Especially with the theme of keeping organized, nothing beats a decent PATH command. PROMPT was only briefly touched upon. Later, in Chapter Eight on ANSI.SYS, you'll see some really neat tricks for spicing up your DOS prompt.

The next chapter deals with two important text files on your system, CONFIG.SYS and AUTOEXEC.BAT. These files are important because they're integral parts of DOS's boot process. Also, they're two files over which you have direct control.

CHAPTER 7

CONFIG.SYS &
AUTOEXEC.BAT

There are five files a PC uses to boot. When you consider how important booting a PC is, how it sets up DOS and configures your system, then you realize how nice it is that the folks who made DOS gave you direct control over two of those five files: CONFIG.SYS and AUTOEXEC.BAT It's not that you're going to spend every day on your PC modifying CONFIG.SYS and AUTOEXEC.BAT. It's that you can.

This chapter is about those two important files on your PC: CONFIG.SYS and AUTOEXEC.BAT. You can change these files to reflect changes in your system, and you can customize them, which lets you tailor the performance of your PC and DOS to your personal tastes. There are three sections that tell you how:

- Working with both
- CONFIG.SYS
- AUTOEXEC.BAT

"Working With Both" covers common ground between CONFIG.SYS and AUTOEXEC.BAT. Since this chapter is about modifying (or creating) those two files, you need to know how it's done before moving on. The other two sections concentrate on the individual duties and potential contents of both CONFIG.SYS and AUTOEXEC.BAT.

WORKING WITH BOTH

CONFIG.SYS and AUTOEXEC.BAT have a lot in common. They're both text files; both are always found in the root directory of your boot disk, they're both files that can be used when you boot your computer; you have direct control over the contents of each; and they're both optional.

Since CONFIG.SYS and AUTOEXEC.BAT are text files, you can edit them using any text editor, such as DOS's EDLIN. You can also use a word processor, but if you do so remember to save the files in the plain text or ASCII format. And COPY CON can be used. But it's not recommended. There's too much detail to these two files to risk their production to COPY CON.

Other than the files' creation and editing, and their similarities, CONFIG.SYS and AUTOEXEC.BAT are extremely different in their setup duties. But from a common ground, know that you have control over both and can change and modify each as needs arise. There are two times this will happen:

- When you do it yourself
- When programs do it for you

As a DOS guru, most of the changes you make to these two files should be done yourself. You should be familiar with CONFIG.SYS and AUTOEXEC.BAT, know their responsibilities and what you personally want out of them. When you change your system, you'll know how to change CONFIG.SYS and AUTOEXEC.BAT to reflect your new situation.

The only other time CONFIG.SYS and AUTOEXEC.BAT get changed is when INSTALL programs do it for you. Some programs assume they know more than you do when it comes to those files. For beginners and the DOS timid, that's fine. Those INSTALL programs will chomp right through your AUTOEXEC.BAT file, creating a new PATH for you and making other "adjustments." They'll also snoop through CONFIG.SYS, making changes there as well. That all sounds pretty nifty, but when you have six applications with six INSTALL programs that are messing around in your files, it can get chaotic.

True, changes to CONFIG.SYS and AUTOEXEC.BAT are often in order. But it just makes sense to do them yourself. This is why it's a good idea to keep personal backup copies of each of them—just for those times when an INSTALL or some other program will make unauthorized changes. (This is covered later in this chapter.)

- One important note: *Changes made to CONFIG.SYS or AUTOEXEC.BAT don't effect your system until you reboot*

This is especially true of CONFIG.SYS. Because it's a part of the boot process, making a change won't have any effect on your system until you reset, and then the new command is executed during the boot process. Since AUTOEXEC.BAT works the same way, changes made to it don't happen until you reset as well.

Before getting into the details, know that both CONFIG.SYS and AUTOEXEC.BAT are optional files. Without them, your system will run just fine. But, unfortunately, DOS will then make certain assumptions about how your PC is configured. And those assumptions aren't usually what's best for your personal situation.

CONFIG.SYS

CONFIG.SYS is DOS's configuration file. It's a text file, composed of special CONFIG.SYS commands and directives that tell DOS how to behave, how much memory to use for disk and file storage, and how to control certain parts of the computer via device drivers. But above all, CONFIG.SYS configures your system.

There are 12 CONFIG.SYS commands, each designed either to configure your system or to load a device driver, which controls some device in the computer (see Figure 16).

There are a lot of CONFIG.SYS commands (well, 12) and they do a variety of things. The good news is that you don't have to use all of them to get the most out of your system. In fact, there are only four that you should really pay attention to:

- BUFFERS
- DEVICE
- FILES
- SHELL

The others are interesting, and they can do neat things for you. (Oh, entire books could be written on working with CONFIG.SYS!) But here, concentration is only made on the above four.

Command	DOS 4 Only?	Function
BREAK	No	Turns Control-Break monitoring on or off
BUFFERS	No	Allocates buffer space for file I/O
COUNTRY	No	Sets date/time/currency formatting information
DEVICE	No	Loads a device driver
FCBS	No	Controls the number of open files for file sharing
FILES	No	Sets the maximum number of open files
INSTALL	Yes	Loads a memory resident program
LASTDRIVE	No	Sets the highest available drive letter
REM	Yes	Allows comments to be inserted
SHELL	No	Sets the location and name of DOS's command interpreter
STACKS	No	Allows you to increase DOS's stack storage space
SWITCHES	Yes	Provides keyboard compatibility

Figure 16: Shown above is a table of CONFIG.SYS commands.

BUFFERS and FILES

The only reason any INSTALL or SETUP program will ever check your CONFIG.SYS file is to see how many FILES and BUFFERS you have set. The general rule is, the more the merrier.

Why? Because a lot of applications, especially databases and accounting packages, rely heavily on disk access. The more FILES and BUFFERS you have allocated, the more quickly those applications can run. So if the values specified aren't high enough, the programs either won't run or will run slowly.

BUFFERS set the number of file buffers DOS uses. The format is:

```
BUFFERS = n
```

Where n is the number of file buffers you'd like DOS to use. It can range from one through 99.

File buffers are areas in memory DOS sets aside for storing information as its read from or written to DISK. Unless otherwise specified, DOS will "give you" from between two to 15 buffers. This normally isn't enough for most applications. So I recommend you set BUFFERS equal to 32. This is done by the following line in your CONFIG.SYS file:

```
BUFFERS = 32
```

FILES is used to specify the maximum number of files DOS can have open at a single time. The format is:

```
FILES = n
```

Where n is the maximum number of files you'll let DOS keep open. It can range from eight to 255. If you don't specify FILES, DOS gives you eight.

As with BUFFERS, FILES should be set to some high value, typically the same value as BUFFERS. Therefore, the following line should be placed in your CONFIG.SYS file:

```
FILES = 32
```

Together, FILES and BUFFERS are the most important part of your CONFIG.SYS file—at least important as far as some heavy disk access applications are concerned.

The only drawbacks to having large values for FILES and BUFFERS is that they use up some memory. BUFFERS uses 528 bytes for each buffer you establish, and FILES uses 48 bytes for each value greater than eight. But that's not bad when you consider how slowly disk access will run if you undercut the values.

DEVICE

CONFIG.SYS's DEVICE command is used to load a device driver. This isn't a required command, but a lot of the PC's add-ons and devices, from extra memory to the CD-ROM, require a DEVICE driver to run. So knowing how to set up one is important.

Device drivers are low-memory programs that control extra devices, specifically those DOS doesn't know about. This allows other programs to access the device without each having to write its own driver.

Device drivers are loaded by the DEVICE command by specifying the driver's pathname after DEVICE= in the CONFIG.SYS file. For example:

```
DEVICE=C:\DOS\ANSI.SYS
```

That line loads the ANSI.SYS device driver into memory. (ANSI.SYS gives extra control to the screen and keyboard.) Note that the device driver has the .SYS filename extension. This is true for all device drivers, though not every file on disk with a .SYS extension is a device driver.

Also, in the above example, note how the full pathname is used to specify the location for ANSI.SYS. Unless you specify a drive letter and path, DOS will assume the device driver to be in the root directory. Since leaving it there is bad organization, it's best to specify the full pathname location of the device driver.

There are many types of device drivers. DOS comes with seven. Most of DOS's device drivers deal with IBM-specific hardware. However, third-party developers have device drivers for a variety of hardware and software setups. But the three most common device drivers found in a CONFIG.SYS file are the following:

- ANSI.SYS
- MOUSE.SYS
- EMS.SYS

ANSI.SYS was covered above. MOUSE.SYS is a mouse device driver, designed to interface a computer mouse to your PC. There are two versions of this driver. One is a memory resident program (usually loaded in AUTOEXEC.BAT) and the other is the device driver, MOUSE.SYS. Of the two, MOUSE.SYS takes up less RAM, so I recommend you use it.

EMS.SYS is an EMS (Expanded Memory System) device driver. It can go by many names, and some of these types of drivers are used to emulate EMS memory in '286 and '386 systems.

Driver Name	Comments
ANSI.SYS	Gives extra control to the screen and keyboard
DISPLAY.SYS	Used with the IBM PC Convertible and laptops to control the screen
DRIVER.SYS	Assign external disk drives a drive letter
PRINTER.SYS	Allows certain IBM printers to access alternative character sets
VDISK.SYS	Sets up a RAM disk
XMAEM.SYS	An Extended Memory Adapter controller for IBM's PS/2 systems (DOS 4 only)

Figure 17: DOS comes equipped with seven DEVICE drivers.

SHELL

As with DEVICE, SHELL isn't an all-important CON-FIG.SYS command, but it does come in handy if you know how to use it. Basically, SHELL's function is to define a command interpreter for DOS. Normally, COMMAND.COM is used. However, SHELL will let you define another one.

The format for SHELL is like DEVICE:

SHELL = *filename*

Filename here is the full pathname of a command interpreter to use for DOS. So far in DOS's life, COMMAND.COM is the most popular command interpreter available. And if a SHELL directive is specified in CONFIG.SYS, DOS will look for COMMAND.COM (in the root directory) and load it.

The most common use of SHELL is to specify a different location for COMMAND.COM—somewhere other than the root directory. For example, if you truly want to keep your root directory clean, you can include the following line in CONFIG.SYS:

SHELL = C:\DOS\COMMAND.COM

This tells DOS to look for the command interpreter (COMMAND.COM in this case) in your DOS subdirectory.

There are other advantages to using the SHELL command in CONFIG.SYS—besides just putting COMMAND.COM elsewhere on your disk. The most important is that you can increase the size of your DOS environment using the SHELL command.

COMMAND.COM, like a few other DOS programs, has optional switches. The two switches available with COMMAND.COM are /P and /E.

The /P switch directs COMMAND.COM to look for and run the AUTOEXEC.BAT file (in the root directory). The /E switch is followed by a colon and the size of your environment in bytes. This is the only way to increase your environment size.

For example, I use the following line in my CONFIG.SYS file:

SHELL=C:\SYSTEM\DOS\COMMAND.COM /E:1024 /P

On my system, I've put COMMAND.COM in my \SYS-TEM\DOS subdirectory. The /E: switch sets my environment size to 1,024 bytes—one "K." The /P switch directs COM-MAND.COM to process my AUTOEXEC.BAT file. If I wanted a smaller environment size, I could specify "E:512." (Remember, DOS gives you 128 bytes, but it's easy to run out of environment space with that amount.)

But before moving on, there is one problem with re-locating COMMAND.COM: Your COMSPEC environment variable will not reflect the new location.

DOS is dumb about COMSPEC. It will always put your COMMAND.COM in the root directory, regardless of where SHELL tells DOS it is. So in your AUTOEXEC.BAT file, you must deliberately set COMSPEC to the new location for COM-MAND.COM.

Why? Because when some programs quit, they need to re-load the *transient* portion of COMMAND.COM from disk. DOS uses the COMSPEC variable to find COMMAND.COM on disk. So you must keep it properly updated.

CONFIG.SYS EXAMPLES

The following are three examples of various CONFIG.SYS files. Each is setup for a specific purpose and customized according to the user's needs. Comments after each tell what's going on.

Example #1

Here is the standard, run-of-the-mill CONFIG.SYS file, applicable to just about any generic PC:

```
1: BUFFERS = 32
2: FILES = 32
3: DEVICE = C:\DOS\ANSI.SYS
```

That's it! BUFFERS and FILES are both set to 32, and the ANSI.SYS device driver is loaded. This will serve just about any PC well. And if you need to add device drivers later, then a simple pass through an editor will do the job.

Example #2

Here is my '386 system's CONFIG.SYS file:

```
1: DEVICE=C:\SYSTEM\DV\QEMM.SYS
2: BUFFERS = 32
3: FILES = 40
4: LASTDRIVE = Z
5: SHELL=C:\SYSTEM\DOS\COMMAND.COM /E:1024 /P
6: DEVICE = C:\SYSTEM\DOS\ANSI.SYS
7: DEVICE = C:\SYSTEM\MOUSE\MOUSE.SYS
```

Three DEVICE drivers are loaded. The first is QEMM.SYS in line 1, which is used with *DESQview/386* (and why it's in the \SYSTEM\DV subdirectory). That driver converts the '386's extended memory into expanded memory for use with *DESQview*.

The other DEVICE commands in lines 6 and 7 load the ANSI.SYS device driver and the Microsoft Mouse device driver, respectively.

Lines 2 and 3 set BUFFERS and FILES equal to 32 and 40. Why so high? I dunno. Some program I loaded at one time wanted values that high, so I set them. A value of 32 for each probably would have been just fine.

The LASTDRIVE command in line 4 sets the highest available drive letter I can use to "Z." This is for use with DOS's SUBST command, which will reassign a subdirectory to a disk drive letter. That makes accessing the subdirectory—or putting on the path—as easy as using a drive letter. For example:

```
SUBST G: C:\GAMES
```

This assigns the drive letter "G" to the subdirectory C:\GAMES. When you type G: at the DOS prompt, or access Drive

G, you'll really be using the \GAMES subdirectory. SUBST really comes in handy for remote and hard to type subdirectories.

Finally, the SHELL command in line 5 is used to set a new location for COMMAND.COM. The environment size is set to 1K and the /P switch runs my AUTOEXEC.BAT file.

Example #3

This is a CONFIG.SYS file for an IBM PC running DOS 4. Note how it uses some DOS 4-only items:

```
1: REM CONFIG.SYS File for Denise
2: REM September 9, 1988
3:
4: FILES = 40
5: BUFFERS = 32,8
6: FILES = 20
7: DEVICE = C:\SYSTEM\DOS\ANSI.SYS
8: DEVICE = C:\SYSTEM\DOS\DRIVER.SYS/D:1/T:80/S:9/H:2/F:;2
```

Note how this CONFIG.SYS file makes use of DOS 4's REM command to insert comments? Also note the blank line 3?

The BUFFERS command with DOS 4 includes an extra parameter, following the number of file buffers and a comma. This parameter specifies a read-ahead value for advance reading of sectors from disk.

Lines 5 and 6 are pretty normal, specifying FILES and the ANSI.SYS device driver. Line 7, though, loads the DRIVER.SYS device driver. On this particular system, a PC/XT, Drive B is a 720K disk drive. The PC/XT's BIOS doesn't understand that, so DRIVER.SYS is necessary to convert the drive into its full 720K format. Though the drive can only be accessed at that level when it's referred to as Drive D. (Weird.)

Aside from the REM/comments and DRIVER.SYS command, this CONFIG.SYS file was originally created by DOS 4's IN-STALL program. Of all the versions of DOS, version 4 finally does it right with a decent INSTALL program.

AUTOEXEC.BAT

AUTOEXEC.BAT is a batch file, but it's the most important batch file you can have on your system. Its primary job is setting up the way COMMAND.COM interacts with you. Where CONFIG.SYS is more on the low-level of DOS, AUTOEXEC.BAT has direct impact to the way you use the machine.

AUTOEXEC.BAT is optional. If you don't write one, DOS simply comes up, asking you for the date and time, and then it dumps you out to the boring old C⟩ prompt.

Things to Put in Your AUTOEXEC.BAT File

There are a lot of things you may want to do in your AUTOEXEC.BAT file. Most people have AUTOEXEC.BAT do one or all of the following:

■ Set the system clock

All today's ATs, '286s, and '386s come with built-in clocks. But older PC/XTs had to have internal clocks added. Those clocks required that a program be run to set DOS's clock to match the real time. That program is usually put in AUTOEXEC.BAT, ensuring that the system has the proper time each time you boot it.

If you don't have a system clock, you can still put DOS's DATE and TIME commands into AUTOEXEC.BAT, which will prompt you to enter the date and time. (DOS won't do it automatically if AUTOEXEC.BAT exists.) However, if you have an AT, '286 or '386, the time is always set and you can skip this step.

■ Set a PATH

The PATH variable is usually set using AUTOEXEC.BAT. You can specify a PATH using the PATH command, or the SET command with "SET PATH=". As with everything done in AUTOEXEC.BAT, this saves you the hassle of having to type it in at the command prompt each time you start your computer.

■ Set a PROMPT

You can also establish a system prompt using the PROMPT command (or "SET PROMPT=") in AUTOEXEC.BAT.

■ Set the screen mode

Some displays require a special screen mode to be set. For example, if you have a Hercules monographics display, you may want to run the HSG setup program to warm up the graphics. If you have two monitors, you may want to use MODE BW80 or MODE Co80 to activate either the monochrome or color monitor, respectively.

■ Set up the printer

Some printers require a setup program to run. Or, if you have a serial printer, you can use the MODE command to reassign it to the PRN device. There are two commands to do this:

```
MODE COM1:9600,N,8,1,P
MODE LPT1=COM1
```

The first line sets the first serial port (COM1) to 9,600 BPS, no parity, 8 data bits, one stop bit, and the Printer mode. The second line reassigns LPT1, the first printer, to COM1, the first serial port.

■ Set a code page

The MODE command can also be used in AUTOEXEC.BAT to assign a code page to your screen or printer. Code pages are used to redefine the Extended ASCII character set, allowing for foreign language character sets or special characters to be used instead of the standard IBM Extended ASCII characters.

■ Change the screen color

Using the ANSI.SYS driver, you can write a line in AUTOEXEC.BAT to assign a new color for the display.

■ SET environment variables

If some applications require an environment variable, they can be assigned in AUTOEXEC.BAT. For example, the *PC*

Paintbrush program uses the environment variable TMP to equal the drive letter of any RAM drive you may have in your system. You could put the following in AUTOEXEC.BAT for your paint program:

```
SET TMP=D
```

This is assuming that Drive D is a RAM disk.

■ Run startup programs

Startup programs could be special utilities to initialize some part of your computer, the network adapter, the CD-ROM drive, or a laser printer. Or they could be memory-resident programs or utilities. A good example would be a daily reminder calendar you may want to inform you of your appointments.

There is no limit (aside from RAM) on the number of startup programs you can stick into AUTOEXEC.BAT.

■ Run applications or shells

Finally, you can end AUTOEXEC.BAT with the name of a program you traditionally run when you first start your PC. For example, if you immediately go into *PC Tool's* PC Shell program, you can end AUTOEXEC.BAT with that. If the first program you run is *DESQview*, you can run that as well. Otherwise, AUTOEXEC.BAT will stop executing and dump you back at the command prompt, which—if you've used your PROMPT command properly—won't be so boring.

AUTOEXEC.BAT EXAMPLES

As with CONFIG.SYS, it helps to see some examples to drive home the point I'm trying to make with what you can do with AUTOEXEC.BAT.

Note that each AUTOEXEC.BAT file traditionally starts with ECHO OFF. If you have DOS 3.3, you can use @ECHO OFF to have a totally "silent" AUTOEXEC.BAT file. Note that the line numbers here are for reference purposes only.

Example #1

Here is a very basic AUTOEXEC.BAT file:

```
1: @ECHO OFF
2: PROMPT $P$G
3: PATH C:\DOS;C:\WP;C:\UTIL
4: RCLK
```

This batch file does three things (besides turning ECHO off): It sets the prompt to the current pathname plus the greater-than; it sets the path to three subdirectories; and it runs RCLK, which is probably a clock-setting program.

Example #2

Going along with my egotistical display of my '386 system's CONFIG.SYS file, here is my AUTOEXEC.BAT file:

```
01: @ECHO off
02: SET COMSPEC=C:\SYSTEM\DOS\COMMAND.COM
03: PROMPT = $p$g
04: PATH=C:\SYSTEM\DOS;C:\SYSTEM\UTIL\;C:\SYSTEM\BATCH
05: SET MASM=/V /Z
06: NUMOFF
07: NDOSEDIT
08: REM Make safety copies of these...
09: COPY \AUTOEXEC.* C:\TEMP ) nul
10: COPY \CONFIG.* C:\TEMP ) nul
11: REM Destroy any Windows temporary files...
12: IF EXIST ~*.* DEL ~*.* ) nul
13: REM *** Quicken's Billminder program **
14: C:\MISC\QUICKEN3\BILLMIND C:\MISC\QUICKEN3
```

Line 1 turns ECHO off.

Line 2 SETs the COMSPEC environment variable to reflect the true location of COMMAND.COM, as reset by the SHELL command in my CONFIG.SYS file. Remember this if you reset COMMAND.COM using SHELL.

Line 3 sets my PROMPT and line 4 sets the PATH to three popular subdirectories. Notice how I use the BATCH file subdirectory to run all files on my system.

Line 5 sets the environment variable MASM for the Microsoft Macro Assembler program.

Lines 6 and 7 run two utilities. The first, NUMOFF, turns off the Num Lock, which is always set on when most AT compatibles boot. The second runs a memory resident program, NDOSEDIT, which allows for better editing at the DOS command prompt.

Lines 8 thought 10 do something I feel is important. Line 8 is a REMark, which tells me that lines 9 and 10 make backup copies of my AUTOEXEC.BAT and CONFIG.SYS files. Both of them are copied to the \TEMP subdirectory, and the output is redirected to the NUL device (which suppresses the "1 File(s) copied" message on the screen).

Why do this? Just in case. Some INSTALL programs may modify my CONFIG.SYS or AUTOEXEC.BAT files—even when I tell them not to. The safety copy of each means that I can get the original back if I need to.

Lines 11 and 12 will remove any temporary files created by Microsoft *Windows*. The IF batch command in line 12 tests for any files starting with a tilde (~), which is *Window's* earmark for a temporary file.

Finally, lines 13 and 14 run *Quicken's* Billminder program.

Note how REM commands were used throughout this AUTOEXEC.BAT file to let me know what each command is doing. REM can also be used to "comment out" certain parts of the file. For example, if I didn't want to run NUMOFF any more, I could change line 6 to read:

```
REM NUMOFF
```

This would keep NUMOFF in the batch file, but the REM command would render it inoperative. At a later date, if I wanted NUMOFF back, I could simply delete the REM and have it back.

Example #3

The following AUTOEXEC.BAT file was created for a PC/XT by DOS 4's INSTALL program:

```
01: @ECHO OFF
02: SET COMSPEC=C:\DOS\COMMAND.COM
03: VERIFY OFF
04: PATH C:\DOS
05: APPEND /E
06: APPEND C:\DOS
07: PROMPT $P$G
08: C:\DOS\GRAPHICS
09: VER
10: PRINT /D:LPT1
11: DOSSHELL
```

This is an interesting and fun AUTOEXEC.BAT to examine because all the choices were made by DOS 4 itself—and they aren't bad choices. Here are the highlights:

Line 2 sets the COMSPEC variable (because the INSTALL program also moves COMMAND.COM via CONFIG.SYS).

The VERIFY OFF in line 3 isn't really necessary, but it does speed up disk access.

Line 4 sets a short path to the DOS subdirectory, DOS hasn't installed any other subdirectories on your system.

Lines 5 and 6 set up the APPEND command. APPEND works like PATH, except it's a search path for data files instead of programs.

Line 7 sets the PROMPT to the standard PG (which makes you wonder why DOS doesn't default to it automatically).

Line 8 runs the DOS GRAPHICS program, which basically provides a graphic character set for the BASIC programming language.

Line 9 displays the DOS version number.

Line 10 activates DOS's memory-resident print spooler program, PRINT.

And finally, line 11 runs the DOS shell program DOSSHELL. This AUTOEXEC.BAT file is interesting, but only because DOS set it up. After mulling over the options, it could easily be pared down to the following:

```
1: @ECHO OFF
2: SET COMSPEC=C:\DOS\COMMAND.COM
3: PATH C:\DOS
4: PROMPT $P$G
5: VER
6: DOSSHELL
```

VERIFY, APPEND, GRAPHICS, and PRINT aren't really necessary. In fact, they take up some memory that could be used for other things in the system. But the choice is really up to you. Put in your AUTOEXEC.BAT file whatever you feel will best service your system.

SUMMARY

This chapter dealt with two very important files that allow you to have direct control over how DOS uses your computer, and how you use DOS.

CONFIG.SYS is DOS's configuration file. It sets up memory storage for DOS to use during disk access, controls various parts of the computer, and allows you to load device drivers. It's those device drivers that expand the capability of DOS.

AUTOEXEC.BAT is the first program COMMAND.COM runs. It can be used for a variety of purposes. Generally, anything you'd normally type at the command prompt when you first start your system can be put into the AUTOEXEC.BAT file.

The only thing missing from these two files are tricks. But don't worry. ANSI.SYS has a lot of tricks up its sleeve. It's covered in the next chapter.

PART FOUR

CHAPTER 8

ANSI.SYS Tricks

One of the most misunderstood and seldom-used goodies that comes with DOS is the ANSI.SYS driver. What it does is give you access to a series of codes that can control your display and keyboard. It's really quite versatile. And you can do amazing stuff with it; boggle the minds of your friends!

This chapter is about ANSI.SYS and what it can do for your system. It's covered here in three parts:

- The ANSI.SYS device driver
- The ANSI codes
- Using ANSI.SYS

There's a lot you can do with ANSI.SYS. Okay, it's cryptic and not too obvious for most users to understand. But once you have it loaded, and then know about the codes and how to use them, your system prompt and batch files will never look the same.

One important note before moving on: ANSI.SYS plays a lot upon color. If you have a color system, you'll really see ANSI.SYS strut its stuff. But don't feel you're left out in the black-and-white if you have monochrome. ANSI.SYS's cursor commands and keyboard reassignment techniques still have plenty to offer you.

THE ANSI.SYS DEVICE DRIVER

ANSI.SYS is a device driver included with every version of DOS. What ANSI.SYS does is to give you access to the ANSI control codes, a commonly defined set of instructions for controlling your screen and keyboard. By loading the ANSI.SYS device driver in your CONFIG.SYS file, DOS and your programs can take advantage of these codes.

ANSI.SYS was included with DOS because IBM and Microsoft originally thought a lot of software would be written directly for DOS. That isn't the case, however. Most PC software is written to the PC's BIOS, or directly to the hardware itself. So ANSI.SYS kind of sits in the dust as far as a required device driver for some applications.

Had IBM and Microsoft been correct, ANSI.SYS would have allowed programs written for DOS to control the cursor, change color, and manipulate information on the screen. These functions are missing from DOS directly, but ANSI.SYS supplies them.

Today, ANSI.SYS isn't used by most people. Few, if any, applications require it. So rather than waste the 1.5K of memory it uses, people don't bother. But with ANSI.SYS installed, you can really spice up batch files and produce interesting prompts, which is covered later in this chapter.

It controls your screen and keyboard by letting you take advantage of ANSI control codes.

To install ANSI.SYS, and take advantage of its features, you add a line such as the following to your CONFIG.SYS file:

```
DEVICE = C:\DOS\ANSI.SYS
```

This assumes ANSI.SYS is in the \DOS subdirectory on Drive C. If your ANSI.SYS file is elsewhere, remember to specify its full path in CONFIG.SYS.

After entering the above line, reboot your system to re-load CONFIG.SYS and let the changes take effect.

THE ANSI CODES

ANSI stands for the American National Standards Institute. It's an institute that defines a number of computer standards, most of which are ignored by mainstream personal computing. (As all information from any committee should be ignored.)

The ANSI.SYS driver uses the ANSI standard codes for controlling the screen and keyboard. These are a series of instructions that do a number of things, most of which are listed below:

- Manipulate the cursor on the display
- Erase a line of text or the entire screen
- Set the graphics mode
- Change the color of text
- Reassign keys and characters on the keyboard
- Other stuff

Basically what the ANSI codes do is give you control that DOS doesn't have directly over the display. There are no DOS commands to "move the cursor up one line" or to change the screen color. ANSI does that for you. (But only if you load the ANSI.SYS driver in CONFIG.SYS.)

ANSI also allows you to reassign keys on the keyboard, plus assign strings of text to certain keys. You can totally re-define the function keys in DOS, having them display strings of text when you press them.

But, before getting all excited, note that the ANSI.SYS driver included with DOS is actually a subset of the complete ANSI command list. There are some missing items. But since no one complains, they've never bothered to upgrade the driver. (Other drivers exist; you should check your local PC user group's library or a software warehouse for other ANSI.SYS-like drivers.)

The ESCape Sequence

ANSI codes themselves are a series of characters, primarily letters, numbers and symbols used to indicate what you want to be done. It's cryptic. In fact, few people get into ANSI because the codes don't make any sense and are hard to memorize (which is why there's Appendix B in this book). The toughest part of all is the prefix for each code, called an *escape sequence*.

All ANSI codes start with an escape sequence. That's the ESC character, code 27 produced by pressing ESC or Control-[, followed by a left bracket, [.

The problem with the escape sequence is the ESC character. Pressing ESC doesn't usually produce that character. Instead, the ESC key could change the mode in your text editor, it could erase a line of text, or it could do a number of things, none of which is to display the ESC character (which looks like "←" on the screen).

But there are solutions.

Quite a few word processors and text editor allow you to enter the ESC character (and other "control" characters) by using a prefix key. In *WordStar* (and other *WordStar*-like editors), the prefix key is Control-P. So to insert an ANSI escape sequence in *WordStar* you would type:

```
Control-P ESC [
```

In *QEdit*, a *WordStar*-like text editor, this produces the following on the screen:

```
← [
```

The Control-P is the "literal prefix," meaning the next character you type will be inserted as-is in the text.

In *WordPerfect*, you can use the Control-V prefix to insert a literal character. To enter the ANSI escape sequence in *Word-Perfect*, type:

```
Control-V ESC [
```

This produces "^[[" on the screen, ^[being the symbol for ESCape. But if you use *WordStar* or *WordPerfect*, remember to save the document in the text-only or ASCII format. Other codes used by word processors may interfere with the ANSI driver's interpretation.

Finally, many text editors have a special prefix key for entering control characters. In EDLIN, DOS's insufferable text editor, the prefix command is Control-V, but it doesn't work like *Word-Perfect*. To enter an ANSI escape sequence in EDLIN, you can type the following:

```
Control-V [ [
```

The Control-V is a control-code character prefix. It inserts a ^V into the document, but it's used to convert the following character into a control code. In this case, [is converted into ^[, which is an ESCape.

Other word processors and text editors have other methods of inserting an ESC character into text. The PROMPT command even has the $e command which puts an ESCape into your system prompt. But don't look for any miracles at the command line. There's no way to enter an escape prefix there—which only means your ANSI tricks are limited to batch files, text files, and the PROMPT command.

ANSI Commands

Following the escape sequence are ANSI commands. There are two types of ANSI commands, those that control your screen and those that control the keyboard.

A complete list of all the ANSI commands available under DOS's ANSI.SYS driver is provided in Appendix B. For reference, here are a few of the more popular ones:

Erase Display

The Erase Display command is used to clear the screen. It has the same results as CLS does. CLS uses the same commands:

← [2J

The escape sequence is followed by 2J, the actual ANSI codes that clear the screen. This is one of the simplest codes.

Position Cursor

The Position Cursor command will move the cursor to any location on the screen. This is handy for precise control of text location in batch files and when building menus. The command is:

← [*row; column*H

Row and *column* are the row and column to which you want the cursor moved. Notice that they're separated by a semicolon and a capital H ends the command. The *row* values range from 1 through 25 for the top through bottom rows. The *column* values range from 1 through 80 for the left to right columns.

Set Graphics Rendition

The Set Graphics Rendition command is the one that sets the colors on your display. Its format is:

← [*n*m

The following *n* values are used only in color monitors to create color text. Note that the value is listed in the table by row and column depending on what color it sets and whether the color is a foreground (text) color or a background color:

You can mix and match the attributes by specifying more than one in the Set Graphics Rendition command. Separate each number by a semicolon and follow the last one with a lower-case M.

For example, to specify bright white letters on a blue background, the following command is used:

← [1;37;44m

n Value	Color	Monochrome
0	Normal	Normal
1	High intensity	High intensity
2	Normal intensity	Normal intensity
4	Blue	Underline
5	Blinking	Blinking
7	Inverse video	Inverse video
8	Invisible	Invisible

Figure 18: Shown above are graphics rendition text attributes.

That command specifies high intensity text (1), white foreground text (37) and blue background (44).

To return the text to standard DOS, plain white on black, low intensity text, use the following:

    ← [0m

Color	Foreground	Background
Black	30	40
Red	31	41
Green	32	42
Yellow	33	43
Blue	34	44
Magenta	35	45
Cyan	36	46
White	37	47

Figure 19: Shown above are graphics rendition text colors.

That resets whatever text colors you've managed to create back to normal.

Making It Work

You know about escape sequences and you've seen some ANSI commands. But how do you get it to work?

ANSI commands must be directed through DOS's console device. In order to get them to work, you have to somehow display them on the screen. In batch files, the ECHO command can be used to do this:

```
ECHO ←[1;37;44m
```

Or ANSI codes can be embedded into a text file. In that case, simply TYPEing the file to the display causes the commands to be executed.

Another alternative is to use the PROMPT command. Prompt allows ANSI escape sequences to be embedded using its $e command. To change the color of your DOS prompt to bright white on blue, you could use the following:

```
PROMPT $e[1;37;44m$p$g
```

The ANSI escape sequence is $e[, $e meaning ESC. The rest of the codes are the ANSI codes to Set Graphics Rendition. And pg sets the prompt to the current path and a greater-than symbol.

A lot of people use PROMPT to get at the ANSI commands. It's the only convenient way to enter them on the command line without resorting to TYPEing a text file or writing batch files. But it's clumsy and fills up the environment needlessly.

USING ANSI.SYS

The following are examples of using ANSI.SYS. They cover the major things ANSI.SYS can do and the different ways you can take advantage of ANSI codes while using your PC.

Menu Text File

A lot of people use batch files to run simple menu systems on their PC. One way to display the menu options is to use endless ECHO commands in a batch file. But that's slow. A better way is to write a text file on disk, then have the batch file TYPE the menu to the screen. If you have ANSI codes in the text file, those will affect the screen as well.

The following text file example displays a color menu in the 40-column mode:

```
←[2J
←[=1h
←[5;15H M A I N   M E N U
←[8;10H 1. Word processing
←[10;10H 2. Spreadsheet
←[12;10H 3. Telecommunications
←[14;15H Enter choice:
```

In this example, the ANSI commands are separated, each on a line by itself. This doesn't have to be the case; ANSI commands can be strung together as long as you like.

Line 1 clears the screen.

Line 2 sets the display mode to 40 columns (for color systems only; refer to Appendix B for more information about this command).

Lines 3 through 7 use the ANSI cursor-positioning commands to position the menu items on the display.

If you wanted a color menu, you should add the color command in line one, before the screen clears. ANSI will then clear the screen with the desired color and all subsequent text will also appear as that color.

To make this file work, it needs to be saved to disk, for example, to MENU.TXT. Then your batch file can just TYPE MENU.TXT or use COPY MENU.TXT CON to make ANSI do its thing.

American Flag Batch File

The following batch file will produce an American flag on your display. (Just don't burn the monitor while this batch file is running.):

```
01: @ECHO OFF
02: REM ANSI American Flag
03: CLS
04: ECHO ←[37;44m* * * * *   ←[41m                    =
05: ECHO ←[37;44m * * * *    ←[47m                    =
06: ECHO ←[37;44m* * * * * *  ←[41m                   =
07: ECHO ←[37;44m * * * *     ←[47m                   =
08: ECHO ←[37;44m* * * * * *  ←[41m                   =
09: ECHO ←[47m                                        =
10: ECHO ←[41m                                        =
11: ECHO ←[47m                                        =
12: ECHO ←[41m                                        =
13: ECHO ←[0m
```

Note: There are 25 spaces after the "m" in lines 4 through 8, and there are 38 spaces following "m" in lines 9 through 12.

In this batch file, lines 4 through 12 use the ANSI codes to set color. First, the foreground color is set to white and the background is set to blue for the field of stars, Lines 4 through 8. Each line ends by resetting the background color to red (41) or white (47) for the stripes in the flag.

Lines 9 through 12 continue setting alternate stripes, red (41) and white (47).

Finally, line 13 resets back to the normal color display.

To run the batch file, save it to disk as FLAG.BAT, then type FLAG at the DOS prompt. Be prepared to stand, salute, and sing patriotic songs.

Spicing Up the Prompt

ANSI commands are placed into the prompt using the $e command. This is most often used to give color to DOS. For example, the following prompt always sets DOS's text colors to bright blue on white:

```
PROMPT $e[1;37;44m$p$g
```

If you prefer other colors, they can be inserted in the prompt as well. But by far, the most complex prompt is the screen update prompt.

The screen update prompt displays the current directory and the date and time at the top of the screen. It makes heavy use of ANSI commands to move and position the cursor, as well as change color. Here's the prompt:

```
PROMPT=$e[s$e[1;1H$e[7m$e[K$p$e[1;45H$d @ $t$e[0m$e[u$g
```

Command	Function
$e[s	Save the current cursor position
$e[1;1H	"Home" the cursor
$e[7m	Set inverse video on
$e[K	Erase that line, set inverse video
$p	Print the current directory and path
$e[1;45H	Move the cursor to just past the midde screen, top row
$d	Display the date
@	Display a space, then the "at" character
$t	Display a space, then the current time
$e[0m	Change the color back to normal video
$e[u	Restore the cursor position
$g	Display a > character, followed by an optional space

Figure 20: To aid in figuring out the above command, here are the individual ANSI and PROMPT commands.

Mondo, eh? But the end effect is nice, and it works in just about every situation. Briefly, the prompt will constantly display the current directory and path, plus the date and time at the top of the screen. The system prompt is then a sole greater than symbol. It's informative and fun to look at. And it's only possible with ANSI.SYS.

Re-assigning Keyboard Characters

ANSI's keyboard control lets you do two things:

- Assign a character to any key on the keyboard
- Assign a string of text to any key on the keyboard

ANSI keyboard reassignment is covered in this section. Assigning a text string is covered in the text.

What ANSI keyboard reassignment does is to replace the character displayed when you press a key with some other character. Note that this only works at the DOS prompt, or with programs that use DOS's functions for input. Normally this excludes all mainstream applications.

For example, you can write a command to cause the █ symbol to be displayed each time you press the * key. Such a command would look like this:

```
@echo ←[42;254p
```

The format for ANSI's Keyboard Key Reassignment is:

```
←[oldkey;newkeyp
```

Oldkey is the ASCII value of the keyboard key you're reassigning. *Newkey* is the ASCII value of the character you want displayed when you press *oldkey*'s key. In the previous example, the asterisk has an ASCII value of 42. The block character has an ASCII value of 254.

Any two keys can be swapped this way. And you can swap any key combination as well, including Shift, Control, and Alt key combos. But there is one drawback. To properly replace function keys and Alt-key combos, you need to know a key's *scan code*. You then use that scan code value instead of the ASCII value when redefining the keyboard.

For example, the scan code value for the Alt-F1 key is 0, 104. (It's two values.) To reassign the letter "G" to Alt-F1, you use the following:

    ← [0;104;71p

This reassigns G, ASCII 71, to the Alt-F1 key, scan code 0, 104.

A list of scan codes for all keys are listed in Appendix C. But life isn't really that difficult. In fact, if you merely want to swap two ASCII characters, you can just put them in quotes. For example:

    ← ["MN"p

The above command causes the character "N" to be produced when you type the M key. Note that this is for upper case only. To re-assign lower case as well, you need to use a second command:

    ← ["mn"p

These commands can be put into a text file that can be TYPEd to the screen, or you can write a batch file that will execute them, changing keys on your keyboard. Such a batch file is described in the next section.

Text to Function Keys

Reassigning a single key requires a bit of head scratching: Exactly what is it good for? But reassigning a whole string of characters to a single key can have lots of uses. That's the second of ANSI's two keyboard reassignment commands, Keyboard String Reassignment.

The format for Keyboard String Reassignment is almost the same as for single key reassignment. The difference is that *newkey* is replaced by a text string in quotes:

    ← [*key*;"*string*"p

Here, *key* is the ASCII code of some character representing a key on the keyboard. *String* is a string of characters that will be displayed when you type that key.

For example, the ASCII code for the + (plus) key is 43. To have the string "Plus" displayed each time you press the + key, you could enter the following command:

```
←[43;"Plus"p
```

Now pressing + is the same as typing Plus. To get the + key back you can use single key reassignment:

```
←[43;43p
```

This is actually a good way to undo any changes done by any of the ANSI key reassignment commands.

But the most beneficial use of this ANSI command is to assign strings of text to your function keys.

DOS only uses function keys F1 through F7 for various commands. (There is a table listed in Chapter Two.) But there are better things to do with those function keys.

Consider the following batch file, which reassigns text strings to the function keys F1 through F10 (remember that list numbers are included only for reference):

```
01: @ECHO off
02: ECHO  ←[0;59;"DIR";13p
03: ECHO  ←[0;60;"COPY "p
04: ECHO  ←[0;61;"DEL "p
05: ECHO  ←[0;62;"CD ";13p
06: ECHO  ←[0;63;"CD ..";13p
07: ECHO  ←[0;64;"CD \";13p
08: ECHO  ←[0;65;"WP";13p
09: ECHO  ←[0;66;"123";13p
10: ECHO  ←[0;67;"DBASE";13p
11: ECHO  ←[0;68;"SCOM";13p
```

Each line uses ANSI keyboard reassignment to assign a string of characters to the function keys F1 through F10. Note how the ECHO command is used to send that command to the display?

The function keys require two values for reassignment. The first is zero, the second is the scan code for the function key. F1 is scan code 59, F2 is scan code 60, and so on. The text string being assigned to that function key then follows the scan code. So F1 is reassigned to the string "DIR," F2 to the string "COPY" and so on.

Note that some function keys (in lines 2, 5, 6, 7, 8, 9, 10 and 11) have their definitions followed by the value 13. That's a carriage return—the ENTER key. So pressing F4 (line 9) produces "123" followed by ENTER.

You can refer to Appendix C for a list of all the function keys and their scan codes.

SUMMARY

This chapter dealt with that well-known yet little used device driver, ANSI.SYS. ANSI.SYS takes advantage of ANSI-defined codes that can be used to control your screen, manipulate the cursor, or to reassign keys on the keyboard.

All ANSI codes start with an escape sequence, which presents the first problem with using ANSI codes—how to enter the ESC character into your word processor. A second problem is how to send the codes to the display. But most word processors do allow you to insert ESCape, and you can use ANSI commands in your system prompt, in batch files or in text files you type to the screen.

There are a lot of tricks you can pull with ANSI.SYS. Another nifty program DOS has that people seldom use is DEBUG. What you can do with DEBUG and what it can do for you is covered in the next chapter.

CHAPTER 9

Using DEBUG

DEBUG is one of the scariest tools Microsoft and IBM are willing to give you with DOS. In the wrong hands, DEBUG can really do some damage. But that's true of any useful tool, from the hammer to the axe. Knowing how to use DEBUG can really save you some time. And since they give it to you with DOS, you might as well know how to use it.

This chapter is about DEBUG. DEBUG is capable of doing three main things: looking at or manipulating your PC's memory, writing or reading raw data to or from disk, and creating COM programs. Those subjects are covered here in four sections:

- About DEBUG
- Looking at memory
- Looking at disk
- DEBUG as assembler/debugger

DEBUG is a powerful tool. But you should be careful with it. This chapter contains no dangerous or system-altering routines. However, if you deviate from the path or try some experiments on your own, it's possible to screw something up. So *guru emptor*.

ABOUT DEBUG

DEBUG is a cryptic program. It's actually a programmer's tool, but even by those standards it's primitive. Like EDLIN, it has stayed virtually the same since its introduction with DOS 1.0. Better types of programs are available to do the same thing, but unless you're into programming, few people bother with them.

DEBUG is a program debugger, as the name implies. Its purpose is to load programs and monitor the way they run. Using DEBUG, you could load a program and see its internal programming instructions and watch how they run and affect other parts of the PC. But that's only one aspect of DEBUG.

DEBUG can also examine memory. You can "peek" at any memory inside your PC to see what's stored there. It's even possible to modify memory directly. And since DEBUG can load raw data from disk into memory, you can modify that data and then save it back to disk. Therefore, in a roundabout way, DEBUG can modify information on disk.

Finally, DEBUG allows you to create programs. But you can only create programs using low-level Assembly language. Even then, DEBUG's mini-assembler mode is quite primitive. It's only good for creating simple programs, and then only if you're well-versed in the cryptic art of Assembly language programming.

Using DEBUG

Unlike some of DOS's programs, DEBUG is more of an application. To start it, you type DEBUG at the command prompt:

```
C:\ DEBUG
-
```

The hyphen is DEBUG's command prompt. At the prompt you enter one of DEBUG's nefariously cryptic commands, which are all listed in the following table.

Note that the commands can be in either upper or lower case.

Command	Function	Format
A	Assembler	a [address]
C	Compare	c [range address]
D	Dump (display)	d [address] l [length]
E	Enter	e [address value(s)]
F	Fill	f [range value(s)]
G	Go	g [=address]
H	Hexarithmatic	h [value value]
I	Input	i [port]
L	Load (from disk)	l [address drive sector 1 sector 2]
M	Move	m [range address]
N	Name	n [filename]
O	Output	o [port value]
P	Proceed	p [address value]
Q	Quit	q
R	Register modify	r [register]
S	Search	s [range value(s)]
T	Trace	t [=address value]
U	Unassemble	u [address] l [length]
W	Write	w [address drive sector 1 sector 2]
XA	EMS Allocate	xa [pages]
XD	EMS Deallocate	xa [handle]
XM	EMS Status	xs

Figure 21: Shown above are DEBUG's commands.

This is complex stuff. Most of it can be understood by following the examples shown in this chapter. But in case you're interested, the following will help you understand which commands do what:

Address is a memory location. It can be specified as a simple offset, or a segment value plus an offset.

Value is either a single byte value or a string of bytes. It can also be a string of text enclosed in double quotes.

Range is two values, the first is a memory location and the second is the length. For example, a range of 100 bytes at memory location 100 would look like this: "100 100." Some commands may use "*llength*" to *specify a range*.

Port is one of the microprocessor's ports.

Register is one of the microprocessor's registers: AX, BX, CX, DX, SP, BP, SI, DI, DS, ES, SS, CS, or IP.

For the disk access commands, *drive* is the number of the disk drive, with Drive A equal to zero, B equal to one, and so on. The two *sector* values are the absolute starting and ending sector numbers for the information to be read from disk. If only one *sector* is listed, then only its 512 bytes of data are loaded at *address*.

The X commands deal with expanded memory. Refer to the DOS 4 technical reference manual if you care about how they function.

Note that all numeric values are specified in *hexadecimal*. That's counting base 16, as opposed to counting base ten, which we humans use. Hexadecimal is just more convenient for computers (more likely computer programmers) to understand. Since this isn't a book on programming or counting systems, the following chart may help you understand how hexadecimal numbers work:

Base Ten: 1 2 3 4 5 6 7 8 9 10 11 12 13 14 15 16
Hexadecimal: 1 2 3 4 5 6 7 8 9 A B C D E F 10

Since Hexadecimal works off of counting base 16, the number "10" in hexadecimal (or "hex") represents 16 of something. The second column only increments by values of 16. So "20" hex is really 32 (2 x 16). In the first column values from one through nine are represented by "1" through "9," but ten through 15 are represented by "A" through "F."

This can get confusing. But don't let it. This chapter will list hex values for all DEBUG commands and explain them in the text.

LOOKING AT MEMORY

DEBUG's command to examine memory is D, for dump. (See? Even though it's cryptic, there's still room enough for humor.) D is followed by an optional *address* value, plus "1" and the length of the data you want to look at. This is just about the most popular of all DEBUG's commands.

To see how all this works, start DEBUG at your DOS prompt. Type DEBUG:

```
C:\> DEBUG
-
```

You'll see the friendly hyphen, letting you know you're comfortably in the DEBUG program. Next, type "D" and press ENTER.

```
1EEE:0100  66 0D 0A 00 90 38 43 6F-6E 74 65 6E 74 20 6F 66   f....8Content of
1EEE:0110  20 64 65 73 74 69 6E 61-74 69 6F 6E 20 6C 6F 73    destination los
1EEE:0120  74 20 62 65 66 6F 72 65-20 63 6F 70 79 0D 0A 00   t before copy...
1EEE:0130  B6 38 49 6E 76 61 6C 69-64 20 66 69 6C 65 6E 61   .8Invalid filena
1EEE:0140  6D 65 20 6F 72 20 66 69-6C 65 20 6E 6F 74 20 66   me or file not f
1EEE:0150  6F 75 6E 64 0D 0A 00 E2-38 25 39 64 20 46 69 6C   ound....8%9d Fil
1EEE:0160  65 28 73 29 20 63 6F 70-69 65 64 0D 0A 00 09 39   e(s) copied....9
1EEE:0170  70 44 25 39 64 20 46 69-6C 65 28 73 29 20 00 22   pD%9d File(s) ."
```

Figure 22: Shown above is an example of a DEBUG dump.

The first column has two four-digit hexadecimal values. The first is the memory segment. The second, preceded by a colon, is the offset within that segment.

The second column contains two groupings of eight two-digit hex values. These are the actual memory locations located at the segment-offset as shown in the first column.

The third column is the most interesting. It shows you an ASCII (text) rendition of the bytes located at the memory segment and offset. In the example, this actually contains some readable text (probably left over from some previously run application).

Remember all values are in hex. Still, it's confusing. But the following example will show you how useful this can be.

Looking at Your Environment

From Chapter Six, you remember that DOS keeps a copy of your environment stored in memory. DOS knows where to find it, and because that information is well documented, we can use DEBUG to locate a copy of your environment in memory.

To find the environment, first make sure you're in DEBUG. (Type DEBUG at the command prompt.) Next, you need to locate what's called a "PSP."

PSP is a program segment prefix. Each time DOS loads a program it creates a 256 byte block of memory. Into that memory DOS puts various information about the system, including what was typed on the command line, any optional filenames, and—important to us—the secret code for finding DOS's environment.

DOS stores the environment in a different location on each computer. The following examples will find the environment on my test computer. If you follow along, the values and addresses you get will be different, but the basic information (the "road map") is still the same.

DOS keeps the PSP at offset zero when you enter DEBUG. It's 100 hex (256 decimal) bytes long. So display those 256 bytes at offset zero, enter the following command at DEBUG's hyphen prompt:

```
D0 L100
```

After pressing ENTER, you'll see 16 lines of text scroll by. These are the memory locations and their contents of your PSP. You may see some recognizable text, or you may just see a bunch of zeros. (Never mind, it's all information for DOS and your program—not meant for you.)

Information about the environment is stored at hexadecimal offset 2C. There are two bytes stored there. Those bytes represent the memory segment inside the PC where a copy of the environment can be found.

You don't have to hunt down offset 2C in the listing on your screen. Instead, you can use the dump command to display only those two bytes for you. Type the following at DEBUG's hyphen prompt:

```
D2C L2
```

This reads, "Display memory at location 2C, List only 2 bytes." For example, see Figure 23.

```
1EEE:0020                                        F3 1A
```

Figure 23: The environment's segment address in your PSP.

The numbers you see will probably be different from those in the figure. Above, the two bytes are F3 and 1A. These bytes represent the segment address of the environment in my system. But one thing still needs to be done before we know what the segment address is.

Intel microprocessors store memory locations backwards. So when you see F3 and 1A at offset 2C, you're not seeing memory address F31A, you're looking at memory address 1AF3. You must reverse the two bytes to get the proper segment value. On my system, that yields 1AF3. For the values you got, reverse them and put them together. For example, if you got:

```
5A 1C
```

Put them together to equal: 1C5A.

That address is actually a segment number, indicating the location of your environment. The memory offset is zero. So to display the contents of your environment, you use the D command as follows:

```
D1AF3:0
```

For your computer, enter the four digits you came up with, followed by a colon and zero. Pressing ENTER will display your environment in memory. For example, see Figure 24.

```
-d1af3:0

1AF3:0000   43 4F 4D 53 50 45 43 3D-43 3A 5C 53 59 53 54 45    COMSPEC=C:\SYSTE
1AF3:0010   4D 5C 44 4F 53 5C 43 4F-4D 4D 41 4E 44 2E 43 4F    M\DOS\COMMAND.CO
1AF3:0020   4D 00 50 52 4F 4D 50 54-3D 24 70 24 67 20 00 41    M.PROMPT=$p$g .A
1AF3:0030   50 41 54 48 3D 43 3A 5C-53 59 53 54 45 4D 5C 44    PATH=C:\SYSTEM\D
1AF3:0040   4F 53 3B 43 3A 5C 53 59-53 54 45 4D 5C 55 54 49    OS;C:\SYSTEM\UTI
1AF3:0050   4C 3B 43 3A 5C 53 59 53-54 45 4D 5C 42 41 54 43    L;C:\SYSTEM\BATC
1AF3:0060   48 00 4D 41 53 4D 3D 2F-56 20 2F 5A 00 42 50 41    H.MASM=/V /Z.BPA
1AF3:0070   54 48 3D 3B 65 3A 5C 62-72 69 65 66 5C 6D 61 63    TH=;e:\brief\mac
```

Figure 24: My computer's environment in memory.

Look familiar? Can you see the COMPSEC variable, and PATH and PROMPT? Granted, typing SET at the DOS prompt is much easier. But this is an exercise in using DEBUG.

At this point you could use DEBUG to modify your environment. But that's a bad idea (and one reason why DEBUG can be dangerous). However, if you really want to modify memory, try the example in the following section:

Poking to the Screen

The most fun you could have with the early computers, the TSR-80s, Pets and Apples, was manipulating display memory. Every character on the screen occupies a one-byte cubbyhole of memory. So the best way to demonstrate how computers use bytes and memory locations was some direct screen manipulation. You can do the same thing with your PC and DEBUG.

On a PC, the screen memory is located either at memory segment B800 or B000. If you have a monochrome display, the screen is at B000. If you have color, the screen is at B800.

Each character on your display uses one byte of memory. So an "A" in the upper-left-hand corner is actually ASCII 65 ("A") in memory location zero at offset B800 (or B000 for monochrome). All characters on the screen are mapped to memory this way.

However, only every other memory location on the screen holds a character. The odd memory locations hold the character's *attribute*. That is, if a character is bright, underlined, red, green, or whatever, that information is held in the odd byte, the byte right next door to the character itself.

Enough with the technical! Let's do something. If you're in DEBUG, quit it by typing the Q command at the hyphen prompt:

```
-Q
```

There you are, back at DOS. Now clear the screen by typing CLS.

Once the screen is clear, enter DEBUG again. (Type DEBUG and press ENTER.) You'll see the happy, friendly hyphen prompt again.

The E command is used to enter bytes directly into memory. It's followed by an address and then values that will be "poked" into memory. And it can also be followed by a string of text.

Type the following at the hyphen prompt—but don't press ENTER yet:

```
EB800:0 "Hello!"
```

If you have a monochrome display, substitute B000 in place of B800 above.

What this command will do is poke (the technical term) the six bytes "Hello!" into your screen's memory. Press ENTER.

Hlo? But it's colorful!

Tragic as it seems, every other byte (character) in "Hello!" was put into the screen display's attribute location. To truly write "Hello!" directly to the screen, you need to supply the attribute bytes as well. Try the following:

```
EB800:0 "Hpeplplpop!p"
```

A lower-case P separates every letter in "Hello!" After pressing ENTER, you'll see "Hello!" displayed at the top of your screen—but in inverse lettering. The character "p" when sent to the attribute byte on the screen produces the inverse attribute.

You can poke to the screen all day long if you like. Try the following:

```
FB800:0 L2000 21 CE
```

That's an F, not an E. The F command fills the display, all 2000 hex bytes, with the values 21 and CE. Isn't computing fun? (And exciting!)

Once again, you can quit DEBUG by pressing Q.

LOOKING AT DISKS

In addition to examining memory, you can use DEBUG to look at raw data on disk. This is a dangerous thing to do, but only if you're foolish with it. In fact, for these examples, you should use an old floppy disk to experiment on. Then you can feel free to experiment without messing anything up.

Before going into DEBUG, grab an old floppy disk (or a new one) and format it in your A drive. Then, copy a few files over to it. Not many, just about two or three in the root directory. For my diskette, I formatted a 360K floppy and copied my COMMAND.COM and CONFIG.SYS files from my hard drive.

Once that's done, type DEBUG at the DOS prompt. Now you're ready to start looking at disks.

The DEBUG commands that deal with disks are L and W. L stands for Load, and W for Write. Normally, when used by themselves, L and W will load or write an assembly program

you're working on in DEBUG. But they can also load or write raw
data to and from disk. It's not the loading that scary—it's the
writing. You must be careful with the W command.

For the L command, the format is:

L*address drive sector1 sector2*

From the disk drive *drive* you'll be loading the sectors starting
at *sector1* through *sector2* at memory location *address*.

What you'll be doing with the L command is loading a number
of sectors from disk and examining them in memory. This is the
safest thing you can do with the L command and DEBUG. The W
command won't be used here, but conceivably you could load
sectors from disk, modify them in memory, and write them back
out to disk using DEBUG.

The following table shows how the first few sectors of a floppy
diskette are organized:

Disk Size	Boot Sector	FAT Tables	Root Directory	Data
360K	0	1-4	5-11	12-
720K	0	1-6	7-13	14-
1.2M	0	1-14	15-28	29-
1.4M	0	1-18	19-32	33-

Figure 25: Shown is floppy diskette sector information.

With your newly formatted or used diskette in your A drive,
you're going to load the first several sectors of it into disk for
examination. This will be done with the load command as follows:

L100 0 0 *x*

Don't type in the command just yet. What it says is to load into
memory starting at location 100 from disk 0 (your A drive), the
sectors starting with sector 0 through sector *x*. For *x* you will

replace the value in the fifth column in the above table, depending on what size disk drive you have. So for a 360K diskette, type:

```
L100 0 0 C
```

"C" is 12 in hexadecimal. The hex values for 15, 30 and 34 are F, 1E and 22, respectively. Type in the proper number for your sized diskette into a similar statement. Press ENTER.

Your disk drive will spin for a second, then the hyphen prompt will return. Those first several sectors of your floppy diskette have now been loaded into memory. You can examine them using the D command.

At the hyphen prompt, type the following:

```
D100 L100
```

What just scrolled on your screen was the floppy disk's boot sector—or rather a copy of it in RAM. You may see some messages, some text, and other things. But mostly it's computer information. One important bit of info at the top of the listing (which scrolled off your screen) is the name and version of DOS under which the diskette was formatted. Type the following:

```
D100 130
```

On my system, I see the following:

```
1EEE:0100  EB 34 90 49 42 4D 20 20-33 2E 33 00 02 02 01 00   .4.IBM  3.3.....
1EEE:0110  02 70 00 D0 02 FD 02 00-09 00 02 00 00 00 00 00   .p..............
1EEE:0120  00 00 00 00 00 00 00 00-00 00 00 00 00 00 00 12   ................
```

Figure 26: Shown are the first several bytes of a diskette's boot structure.

Clearly visible (in the ASCII column) are the words IBM 3.3. That diskette was formatted under PC-DOS version 3.3.

There are other areas of the disk you can examine, now that
they're in memory. For example, at memory location B00 is the
copy of my diskette's root directory. To see it, I can type:

    DB00

AUTOEXEC.BAT and CONFIG.SYS are displayed just as
they're stored in the root directory.

If you have a different-sized diskette, you'll have to fiddle with
the D command to locate your root directory in memory. But keep
pressing D and eventually it will scroll by.

```
1EEE:0B00  41 55 54 4F 45 58 45 43-42 41 54 20 00 00 00 00   AUTOEXECBAT ....
1EEE:0B10  00 00 00 00 00 00 8C 80-70 14 02 00 4E 04 00 00   ........p...N...
1EEE:0B20  43 4F 4E 46 49 47 20 20-53 59 53 20 00 00 00 00   CONFIG  SYS ....
1EEE:0B30  00 00 00 00 00 00 91 7B-73 14 04 00 B9 00 00 00   .......{s.......
1EEE:0B40  00 00 00 00 00 00 00 00-00 00 00 00 00 00 00 00   ................
1EEE:0B50  00 00 00 00 00 00 00 00-00 00 00 00 00 00 00 00   ................
1EEE:0B60  00 00 00 00 00 00 00 00-00 00 00 00 00 00 00 00   ................
1EEE:0B70  00 00 00 00 00 00 00 00-00 00 00 00 00 00 00 00   ................
```

Figure 27: Shown is the root directory as stored in RAM.

If you're really gutsy, you can modify the diskette and write
its contents back out to disk. But this subject isn't covered here
because of the potential consequences.

To quit DEBUG, type Q at the hyphen prompt.

DEBUG AS ASSEMBLER/DEBUGGER

DEBUG can also be used to create programs, as well as
loading them from disk to examine how they work.

To create a program in DEBUG, you need to know a bit about
how to program the PC—specifically how to program it in assembly language. Rather than tutor you on that here, the following
instructions will create an assembly language program and save it
to disk, all using DEBUG.

Creating READKEY.COM

DEBUG can create COM programs because it has a built-in assembly language program system. There are four steps to creating a COM program (aside from knowing what you want to do in the first place).

1. Enter the assembly language instructions
2. Find the length of the file and set it in the CX register
3. Name the file
4. Write it to disk

The file you're going to create is called READKEY.COM. What it does is to scan the keyboard for input, waiting for a key to be pressed. When a key is pressed, its ASCII value is then returned as an ERRORLEVEL code. That way, you can use READKEY in a batch file to accept keyboard input and act on it using the IF ERRORLEVEL evaluation.

The assembly language instructions for READKEY.COM are as follows:

```
mov ah,1      ;DOS read key function
int 21h       ;Call DOS
mov ah,4Ch    ;DOS quit function
int 21h       ;Call DOS
```

The program is only four lines long—simple by PC standards. But it still appears baffling to you if you're not used to assembly language, or any programming for that matter. Don't worry.

To write this program in DEBUG, enter DEBUG and use the A command to start assembling. Type A at the hyphen prompt.

```
-A
```

```
1EEE:0100
```

DEBUG comes back with a segment and offset. Your segment value will be different from the 1EEE I got, but the second value of 0100 will be the same. DEBUG is now ready for you to enter the assembly language instructions, the instructions listed above.

To create the program, type in each of the following four lines *exactly* as listed here. Press ENTER after each line:

```
MOV AH,1
INT 21
MOV AH,4C
INT 21
```

After the last line, press Control-C to cancel the assembly mode. You'll be returned to the hyphen prompt.

The four lines of assembly code have now been entered into the computer. DEBUG has translated them into the machine instructions that will carry out the task required. But you still need to save it off to disk.

To save the file to disk, you first need to know how long it is. There are ways to figure this out when you're "hand assembling" on your own, but to save you time, the file is only eight bytes long. To communicate this to DOS, you need to change the contents of the microprocessor's CX register to 8. Type the following:

```
RCX
```

DEBUG responds by displaying the current value of the CX register and a colon prompt. Type 8 at the prompt and press ENTER:

```
CX 0000
:8
```

The hyphen prompt returns.

Now you need to give the file a name. The N command is used to name a file. At the hyphen prompt, type N followed by the name of the file, READKEY.COM:

```
N READKEY.COM
```

Press ENTER.

Finally, to write the file to disk, use the W command by itself at the hyphen prompt:

```
W
```

After pressing ENTER, DEBUG comes back with:

```
Writing 0008 bytes
```

The file is now created and sitting on disk. Quit DEBUG (with Q) and at the DOS prompt type DIR to see your new file. You can even test it to make sure it works properly (it does).

DEBUG can also load programs from disk, allowing you to see how they work and disassemble them. This is where the subject really starts to get complex, but feel free to experiment on your own. Just don't use the W command to write any changed files back to disk. Also, note that DEBUG only loads COM files properly.

An Example Using I/O Redirection

When most people use DEBUG, they use it via a batch file and I/O redirection. The DEBUG commands are given to DEBUG via input redirection. This allows DEBUG to be used with a minimum of hassle and mistakes, and it all happens quite quickly.

The following batch file uses DEBUG to reboot your computer. It uses I/O redirection to supply input for DEBUG, but it does it in a unique way.

To reboot a PC, you need to execute the programming instructions found at memory segment FFFF, offset zero. This can be done in DEBUG by typing the following at the hyphen prompt:

```
G=FFFF:0
```

But only type that in if you really want to reset your computer!

Instead of resorting to that, the following batch file uses DEBUG via I/O redirection to reboot your computer.

```
01: GOTO BEGIN
02:
03: RCS
04: FFFF
05: RIP
06: 0000
07: G
08:
09: :BEGIN
10: DEBUG  < REBOOT.BAT
```

Type in this program (using a text editor) and save it to disk
as REBOOT.BAT. Now typing REBOOT at your command
prompt will reboot your computer. Here's how it works:

Line 1 branches batch file execution to the BEGIN label at line
9. Then, line 10 is executed, which runs DEBUG but supplies the
input for DEBUG from the file, REBOOT.BAT.

Lines 3 through 7 are really DEBUG instructions—input for
DEBUG saved in the batch file. What I/O redirection will do is
force all these lines, plus their carriage returns, into DEBUG one
at a time.

The first line, "GOTO BEGIN" is ignored by DEBUG. It
produces an error. Line 2 is blank, which causes DEBUG to skip
past the error message. Then, starting with line 3, the instructions
are passed to DEBUG one at a time as follows:

```
RCS  Reset the Code Segment register
FFFF The new address for the Code Segment
RIP  Reset the Instruction Pointer register
0000 The new address for the Instruction Pointer
G    Go!
```

This has the same effect as typing G=FFFF:0. It causes the computer to start executing the instructions there, which just happen to be the instructions to reboot your PC.

The rest of the batch file isn't executed because the computer is busy re-booting.

SUMMARY

DEBUG is a complex and cryptic program, but as this chapter shows you, it can be extremely useful. You can use DEBUG to look at or modify memory, to load sectors from disk into memory for modification, and to create or modify programs on disk.

DEBUG is useful. But its awkward interface and potential danger keeps a lot of people from using it. Actually, it's more of a toy than anything. Other, better tools (utilities) exist to help you look at programs and examine and fix disks. You should use them rather than risk the consequences of messing something up with DEBUG.

This also wraps up the book on DOS Secrets. There are many more secrets to using DOS than the few described in these pages. But as a budding DOS guru, you now know where to look for them. And once you find a new secret, remember to fiddle with it; find out new ways to apply it. That's the only way you'll ever graduate into true Guruhood.

Good luck!

APPENDICES

APPENDIX A

ASCII

CONTROL CHARACTERS

0 ^@	1 ^A	2 ^B	3 ^C	4 ^D	5 ^E	6 ^F	7 ^G
8 ^H	9 ^I	10 ^J	11 ^K	12 ^L	13 ^M	14 ^N	15 ^O
16 ^P	17 ^Q	18 ^R	19 ^S	20 ^T	21 ^U	22 ^V	23 ^W
24 ^X	25 ^Y	26 ^Z	27 ^[	28 ^\	29 ^]	30 ^^	31 ^_

STANDARD TEXT CHARACTERS

32	33 !	34 "	35 #	36 $	37 %	38 &	39 '
40 (	41)	42 *	43 +	44 ,	45 -	46 .	47 /
48 0	49 1	50 2	51 3	52 4	53 5	54 6	55 7
56 8	57 9	58 :	59 ;	60 <	61 =	62 >	63 ?
64 @	65 A	66 B	67 C	68 D	69 E	70 F	71 G
72 H	73 I	74 J	75 K	76 L	77 M	78 N	79 O
80 P	81 Q	82 R	83 S	84 T	85 U	86 V	87 W
88 X	89 Y	90 Z	91 [	92 \	93]	94 ^	95 _
96 `	97 a	98 b	99 c	100 d	101 e	102 f	103 g
104 h	105 i	106 j	107 k	108 l	109 m	110 n	111 o
112 p	113 q	114 r	115 s	116 t	117 u	118 v	119 w
120 x	121 y	122 z	123 {	124		125 }	126 ~	127 ⌂

EXTENDED ASCII CHARACTERS

128 Ç	129 ü	130 é	131 â	132 ä	133 à	134 å	135 ç
136 ê	137 ë	138 è	139 ï	140 î	141 ì	142 Ä	143 Å
144 É	145 æ	146 Æ	147 ô	148 ö	149 ò	150 û	151 ù
152 ÿ	153 Ö	154 Ü	155 ¢	156 £	157 ¥	158 ₧	159 ƒ
160 á	161 í	162 ó	163 ú	164 ñ	165 Ñ	166 ª	167 º
168 ¿	169 ⌐	170 ¬	171 ½	172 ¼	173 ¡	174 «	175 »
176 ▒	177 ▓	178 █	179 │	180 ┤	181 ╡	182 ╢	183 ╖
184 ╕	185 ╣	186 ║	187 ╗	188 ╝	189 ╜	190 ╛	191 ┐
192 └	193 ┴	194 ┬	195 ├	196 ─	197 ┼	198 ╞	199 ╟
200 ╚	201 ╔	202 ╩	203 ╦	204 ╠	205 ═	206 ╬	207 ╧
208 ╨	209 ╤	210 ╥	211 ╙	212 ╘	213 ╒	214 ╓	215 ╫
216 ╪	217 ┘	218 ┌	219 █	220 ▄	221 ▌	222 ▐	223 ▀
224 α	225 ß	226 Γ	227 π	228 Σ	229 σ	230 µ	231 τ
232 Φ	233 Θ	234 Ω	235 δ	236 ∞	237 φ	238 ∈	239 ∩
240 ≡	241 ±	242 ≥	243 ≤	244 ⌠	245 ⌡	246 ÷	247 ≈
248 °	249 ∙	250 ·	251 √	252 ⁿ	253 ²	254 ■	255

CONTROL CHARACTER NAMES

0	^@	NUL	Null
1	^A	SOH	Start of Heading
2	^B	STX	Start of Text
3	^C	ETX	End of Text
4	^D	EOT	End of Transmission
5	^E	ENQ	Enquiry
6	^F	ACK	Acknowledge
7	^G	BEL	Bell
8	^H	BS	Backspace
9	^I	HT	Horizontal Tab
10	^J	LF	Line Feed
11	^K	VT	Vertical Tab
12	^L	FF	Form Feed
13	^M	CR	Carriage Return
14	^N	SO	Shift Out
15	^O	SI	Shift In

16	^P	DLE	Data Link Escape
17	^Q	DC1	Device Control 1
18	^R	DC2	Device Control 2
19	^S	DC3	Device Control 3
20	^T	DC4	Device Control 4
21	^U	NAK	Negative Acknowledgement
22	^V	SYN	Synchronous File
23	^W	ETB	End of Transmission Block
24	^X	CAN	Cancel
25	^Y	EM	End of Medium
26	^Z	SUB	Substitute
27	^[	ESC	Escape
28	^\	FS	Form Separator
29	^]	GS	Group Separator
30	^^	RS	Record Separator
31	^_	US	Unit Separator

APPENDIX B

ANSI.SYS Commands

The following tables list all the ANSI commands by function. They're presented in the following order:

- Screen commands
- Cursor commands
- Keyboard commands

When describing the escape sequence for each command, note that all characters listed are text character, not numbers. And there is a difference between upper and lower case. If the escape sequence requires an "H," you cannot substitute "h." Also, note that the lower-case L is not a number.

Note that ← represents the ESC character.

SCREEN COMMANDS

The Set Graphics Rendition Command is the one that changes the color of the screen. The value of *n* can be one of the following:

n Value	Attribute	*n* Value	Attribute
0	Normal text	34	Blue foreground
1	High-intensity	35	Magenta foreground
2	Low-intensity	36	Cyan foreground
4	Underline on (mono-chrome display only)	37	White foreground
		40	Black background
5	Blinking on	41	Red background
7	Inverse video on	42	Green background
8	Invisible text	43	Yellow background
30	Black foreground	44	Blue background
31	Red foreground	45	Magenta background
32	Green foreground	46	Cyan background
33	Yellow foreground	47	White background

Figure 28: Shown above are the values of n *and its attributes.*

You can combine two or more attributes to create color combinations. The format is:

[*n* ; *n*m

Separate all values of the variable by a semicolon and end it with a lower-case M.

n Value	Attribute	*n* Value	Attribute
0	Monochrome text, 40x25	6	High-resolution graphics (two color), 640x200
1	Color text, 40x25		
2	Monochrome text, 80x25	14	Color graphics, 640x200
3	Color text, 80x25	15	Monochrome graphics, 640x350
4	Medium-resolution graphics (four color), 320x200	16	Color graphics, 640x350
		17	Color graphics, 640x480
5	Same 4, but with color burst disabled	18	Color graphics, 640x480
		19	Color graphics, 320x200

Figure 29: Shown above are the values of n *for the Set/Rest Mode command.*

ANSI Command	ESC Sequence	Description
Character Wrap On	←[=7h	Wrap characters at 80 columns
Character Wrap Off	←[=7l	Do not wrap characters
Erase Display	←[2J	Clear screen
Erase Line	←[K	Erase from the cursor's position to the end of the line
Set Graphics Rendition	←[*n*m	Change the foreground/background colors on the screen
Set/Reset Mode	←[*n*h	Change the screen resolution and graphics

Figure 30: ANSI screen control commands.

ANSI Command	ESC Sequence	Description
Locate Cursor	←[*row;col*H	Move cursor to row/column
Position Cursor	←[*row;col*f	Move cursor to row/column
Move Cursor Up	←[*n*A	Move cursor up *n* lines
Move Cursor Down	←[*n*B	Move cursor down *n* lines
Move Cursor Right	←[*n*C	Move cursor right *n* columns
Move Cursor Left	←[*n*D	Move cursor left *n* columns
Save Cursor Position	←[s	Store the cursor's current position
Restore Cursor Position	←[u	Restore the cursor's previously sorted position

Figure 31: ANSI cursor control commands.

ANSI Command	ESC Sequence	Description
Keyboard Key Reassignment	←[*oldkey;newkey*p	Reassign the character *newkey* to the keyboard character *oldkey*
Keyboard String Reassignment	←[*oldkey;*"*string*"p	Assign the characters string to the key *oldkey*

Figure 32: ANSI keyboard control commands.

Refer to Chapter Eight for additional information on keyboard reassignment.

APPENDIX C

Keyboard Scan Codes

The following are *scan codes* generated by your keyboard each time you press a key. These codes can be interpreted by several programs, including the ANSI.SYS console driver to reassign keys on the keyboard.

GENERAL SCAN CODES

Code	Key
======	=====
1	Escape
2	1 !
3	2 @
4	3 #
5	4 $
6	5 %
7	6 ^
8	7 &
9	8 *
10	9 (
11	0)
12	- _
13	= +
14	Backspace

15	Tab
16	Q
17	W
18	E
19	R
20	T
21	Y
22	U
23	I
24	O
25	P
26	[{
27	] }
28	ENTER
29	Control key
30	A
31	S
32	D
33	F
34	G
35	H
36	J
37	K
38	L
39	; :
40	' "
41	` ~
42	Left shift key
43	\	
44	Z
45	X
46	C
47	V

48	B
49	N
50	M
51	,
52	.
53	/ ?
54	Right shift key
55	* Print Screen
56	Alt key
57	Spacebar
58	Caps Lock
59	F1
60	F2
61	F3
62	F4
63	F5
64	F6
65	F7
66	F8
67	F9
68	F10
69	Num Lock
70	Scroll Lock
71	Home 7 (keypad numbers only)
72	Up arrow 8
73	PgUp 9
74	- (keypad minus key)
75	Left arrow 4
76	5 (keypad only)
77	Right arrow 6
78	+ (keypad plus key)
79	End 1
80	Down arrow 2

81   PgDn 3
82   Insert key
83   Delete key
84   SysRq
87   F11
86   F12

FUNCTION KEY SCAN CODES

The extended scan codes for the function keys are as follows:

	Normal	Shifted	Control	Alt
F1	0;59	0;84	0;94	0;104
F2	0;60	0;85	0;95	0;105
F3	0;61	0;86	0;96	0;106
F4	0;62	0;87	0;97	0;107
F5	0;63	0;88	0;98	0;108
F6	0;64	0;89	0;99	0;109
F7	0;65	0;90	0;100	0;110
F8	0;66	0;91	0;101	0;111
F9	0;67	0;92	0;102	0;112
F10	0;68	0;93	0;103	0;113

APPENDIX D

Where to Get More Information

You can't learn everything there is to know about DOS in a day. And the information in this book did concentrate on secrets, little-known stuff, seldom-used tricks. Therefore, you need some other place to turn to, some source where you can get other information, from the basics to the hardcore details.

LOCATING SECRET SOURCES

These sources will help you complete your DOS education. Most DOS gurus will spend a lifetime gathering these tips, buying books, and listening to other DOS gurus. Remember—DOS gurus never quibble with each other over minor points. If you know the other guy is wrong, then he's wrong; no need to smash his ego.

The best book on DOS is your DOS manual (believe it or not). Everyone should have a DOS manual, even though some computer stores "install" DOS for you and never give you the manual.

Aside from your DOS manual, another handy reference is *The MS-DOS Encyclopedia*. While it's a hefty and expensive book, it's worth every ounce and every cent. Alone this book replaces half a dozen others on my shelf. If you're serious about DOS, it can't be beat.

For good information on batch file programming and general hard disk management, look into *Advanced MS-DOS Batch File Programming* by myself, available from TAB books. A general purpose guide, *Hard Disk Management*, is available from Prentice Hall, but you'll have to look in a community college bookstore to find it.

For those willing to dive into the bits and bytes of assembly language programming, the following three books are recommended: The Waite Group's *Assembly Language Primer for the IBM PC & XT* (by Robert Lafore), Ray Duncan's *Advanced MS-DOS*, Rector and Alexy's *The 8086 Book*, and the documentation for Microsoft's Macro Assembler. This information is a little advanced and only the seriously foolish should venture into an area as scary as assembly language programming.

Here's the bibliographical information if you're into that sort of thing:

Duncan, Ray, *Advanced MS-DOS*, Washington: Microsoft Press, 1986. ISBN 0-914845-77-2.

Duncan, Ray et al, *The MS-DOS Encyclopedia*, Washington: Microsoft Press, 1988. ISBN 1-55615-049-0.

Gookin, Dan, *Advanced Batch File Programming*, Pennsylvania: TAB Books, 1989. ISBN 0-8306-3197-6.

Gookin, Dan, *Hard Disk Management*, New Jersey, Prentice Hall, 1990. ISBN 0-13-383738-6.

Lafore, Robert, *Assembly Language Primer for the IBM PC & XT*, Virginia: Plume/Waite, 1984. ISBN 0-452-25711-5.

Rector/Alexy, *The 8086 Book*, California: Osborne/McGraw-Hill, 1980. ISBN 0-931988-29-2.

MAGAZINES AND GAZETTES

Aside from these hard-bound sources, there are a few magazines you may want to look into. The best PC magazine for DOS gurus is *PC Resource*. It contains technical information, reviews of products you can afford, tutorials, and programming information.

Coming in second is the popular *PC Magazine*. It comes out once every two weeks, except in July and August. The magazine is composed almost totally of product reviews, though they tend to be products you can't afford. *PC Magazine*'s typical reader is the MIS manager for a Fortune 500 company. It's not written to the individual user (though we buy it in droves). *PC Magazine* also has the most top-notch columnists and runs occasionally informative features that can't be beat.

A good industry magazine to read is *PC Week*, which comes out weekly from most of the same people who make *PC Magazine*. *PC Week* is a little harder to get, however. Basically, it's a free industry publication. However, when "end users" want to pick up a subscription it costs $120/year. You can make an attempt to fill out the free subscription card to see if you qualify. If you're in charge of the office computer system, or are a private consultant, you may "win" the subscription. If so, this is the best up-to-date industry magazine.

Other magazines include *PC World*, which is a general purpose PC magazine but inconsistent in its content. And there's *PC Computing*, which they like to call the "Vanity Fair" of computer magazines.

But there are always sources for information out there. Magazines are the quickest source. And after a few months, the good (and reliable) information usually finds its place in a book.

Other Books From
Computer Publishing Enterprises:

PC Secrets
*Tips and Tricks to Increase Your
Computer's Power*
by R. Andrew Rathbone

Future Computer Opportunities
*Visions of Computers Into
the Year 2000*
by Jack Dunning

Software Buying Secrets
by Wally Wang

DOS Secrets
by Dan Gookin

101 Computer Business Ideas
by Wally Wang

Digital Dave's Computer Tips and Secrets
*A Beginner's Guide to
Problem Solving*
by Roy Davis

The Best FREE Time-Saving Utilities for the PC
by Wally Wang

How to Get Started With Modems
by Jim Kimble

How to Make Money With Computers
by Jack Dunning

Rookie Programming
*A Newcomer's Guide to
Programming in BASIC, C,
and Pascal*
by Ron Dippold

Hundreds of Fascinating and Unique Ways to Use Your Computer
by Tina Rathbone

The Computer Gamer's Bible
by R. Andrew Rathbone

Beginner's Guide to DOS
by Dan Gookin

Computer Entrepreneurs
*People Who Built Successful
Businesses Around Computers*
by Linda Murphy

How to Understand and Buy Computers
By Dan Gookin

Parent's Guide to Educational Software and Computers
by Lynn Stewart and
Toni Michael

The Official Computer Widow's (and Widower's) Handbook
by Experts on Computer
Widow/Widowerhood

For more information about these books, call 1-800-544-5541.

INDEX